Born in Crisis
and
Shaped by Controversy

Born in Crisis

and

Shaped by Controversy

The Relevant History of Methodism

Volume 1
Born in Crisis

JOHN R. TYSON

CASCADE *Books* · Eugene, Oregon

BORN IN CRISIS AND SHAPED BY CONTROVERSY
The Relevant History of Methodism, Volume 1: Born in Crisis

Cascade Books
An Imprint of Wipf and Stock Publishers
199 W. 8th Ave., Suite 3
Eugene, OR 97401

www.wipfandstock.com

PAPERBACK ISBN: 978-1-7252-8132-5
HARDCOVER ISBN: 978-1-7252-8133-2
EBOOK ISBN: 978-1-7252-8134-9

Cataloguing-in-Publication data:

Names: Tyson, John R., author.

Title: Born in crisis and shaped by controversy : the relevant history of methodism,
    volume 1 : born in crisis / John R. Tyson.

Description: Eugene, OR : Cascade Books, 2022 | Includes bibliographical references
    and index.

Identifiers: ISBN 978-1-7252-8132-5 (paperback) | ISBN 978-1-7252-8133-2 (hardcover)
    | ISBN 978-1-7252-8134-9 (ebook)

Subjects: LCSH: Methodism—History—18th century.

Classification: BX8231 .T97 2022 (paperback) | BX8231 .T97 (ebook)

VERSION NUMBER 070722

Contents

Preface

WRITING SOMETIMES FEELS LIKE a solitary endeavor, but actually it is not. I have become convinced that writing—at least informed writing—is done in community; in much the same way that it is said that "it takes a village to raise a child" it also takes a community to birth a book. I am deeply grateful that I have had a diverse community of friends and colleagues who have helped me "raise" this examination of the Methodist religious tradition. I hope that much of what is chronicled in this study will apply, by extrapolation, to other communities of faith, but since I am and have always been a Methodist, it seems best to write about my own tribe.

In the midst of the social, economic, and political crises swirling all around us, I found myself once again drawn toward my Methodist roots and what I found there reminded me that people of deep faith, including the Methodists, have always been challenged and motivated by Christian concern and compassion to try and address the crises of their day. This was certainly true of the extraordinary women and men of faith who were our forerunners, and it can be true for us as well. My recollection of the early Methodists gave me both the hope and resolve to name the crises that so adversely shape the lives of God's people, and to find ways to help alleviate them. This is in our DNA both as Methodists and as people of Christian faith. In a similar way, it breaks my heart to acknowledge that our Methodist family of churches is riven by controversies that have too often divided us, and even now we stand on the edge of a very painful denominational divorce. But our history tells me that we have always cared so deeply about important spiritual, theological, and ecclesiastical issues that contentions have arisen among us about them. Sometimes these controversies have resulted in separations and schisms that have injured or broken the body of Christ in the world. Our history tells me (us) that with God's help we have journeyed on as faithfully as we could in spite of these controversies and contentions. And with God's help we have (hopefully) learned something more about God and about ourselves in that process. For these reasons, I offer this recollection and retelling of the saga of "the people called Methodists" (John Wesely's term), who were (are) a movement of Christians that was *Born in Crisis* (volume 1) and *Shaped by Controversy* (volume 2), with fervent hope and a prayer for a brighter future for the Methodists and for all people who strive to walk the redemptive path of faith and love in our troubled and broken world.

The "village" that gratefully stands behind these volumes includes the clergy and laity who participated in various parts of this journey with me through the several retreats held at Camp Asbury, Casowasco, and Sky Lake, or the "district days" hosted by the Binghamton, Cornerstone, and Northern Flow UMC Districts, where some of these ideas were road-tested. I am also grateful to my colleagues who took classes with me at Colgate Rochester Crozer Divinity School, or the UMC Course of Study where many of these inquiries were born, examined, and refined. I also appreciate the wonderful opportunity given me by the clergy and laity of Asbury First UMC, Covenant UMC, and Webster UMC, all in Rochester, New York, to walk and talk through several of these Crises and Controversies in conversation with them. And finally, I am deeply indebted to ministerial friends and colleagues who read, discussed, and helped me improve various sections of this manuscript. Among these are: Rev. Hannah Bonner, Dr. Richard Hays, Dr. Ann Kemper, Rev. Rick La Due, Ms. Pat Lunn, Dr. Marvin McMickle, Dr. Angela Sims, and others whom I might have forgotten. Obviously, however, the opinions, judgments, and shortcomings herein are entirely my own.

Introduction

THE METHODIST STORY HAS been studied and told in many ways, and from diverse points of view. We have had our fair share of character studies plumbing the lives of the Wesleys, and other notable people on the Methodist family tree. Several good institutional histories have expanded stories of individuals into the saga of a denomination and an entire tradition. But most of these studies have been told from the "inside." They were built out of the cherished family memories, stories, and records that chronicle how a movement of less than a dozen ardent individuals became an international Christian tradition with millions of adherents.

But there is another side to this story, and it comes from the "outside." It comes to us with the potent reminder that Methodism was born as a spiritual, religious, and humanitarian reply to a series of disturbing crises that arose in the English eighteenth century. This religious reply was made by gifted, but also flawed, women and men—a few of whom were named "Wesley." Methodism has been, from its very inception, a movement shaped by mission to a troubled, painful, and dysfunctional world. In that context, Methodists sought to live out Jesus' injunction to "love God with all your heart, mind, and soul and to love your neighbor as yourself" (Matt 22:37–38), as Jesus' call crystalized into the Wesleyan conception of Christian perfection. The movement's mission was, in the well-considered words of John Wesley, "to reform the nation, particularly the Church; and to spread scriptural holiness over the land."[1]

Among the crises that convulsed Georgian England were: 1) the debilitating effects of the political use of religious authority; 2) the challenges of keeping faith in an age of science and reason; 3) the lethargy and decline of "main line" religion; 4) the painful and oppressive impact of class privilege; 5) the inequities caused by dramatic economic disparity; 6) the hopelessness of wage slavery; 7) the devaluing and structural exclusion of women;

---

1. J. Wesley, *Works*, VIII: "Large Minutes," 299.

8) racial prejudice, and the systematic oppression of nonwhite people; 9) the social crisis caused by religious prejudice; and 10) the hurtful effects of debilitating popular culture and its pastimes. These historic crises drew from the early Methodists theological and organizational impulses that became part of their spiritual DNA, and they left them with family traits that have come down to us in this very day. Early Methodism's encounter with and response to these ten crises will be explored in the chapters that follow: 1) "'Don't Let Them Pull the Wool Over Your Eyes': The Crisis of Mixing Religion & Politics; 2) "'A Reasonable Enthusiast': The Challenge of Being a Person of Faith in the Age of Reason"; 3) "'Awake Thou That Sleepest': The Crisis of Ecclesiastical Slumber and Dysfunction"; 4) "'The Most Class-ridden Country under the Sun': The Crisis of Class and Privilege"; 5) "'Help Me Make the Poor My Friends': The Crisis of Economic Disparity"; 6) "'The Methodists are a Low, Insignificant People': The Crisis of the Working Poor"; 7) "'Like a Mother in Israel': The Crisis of Women's Inequality and Exclusion"; 8) "'Give Liberty to Whom Liberty Is Due': The Crisis Caused by Racial Prejudice"; 9) "'Just Enough Religion to Make Us Hate': The Crisis Caused by Religious Prejudice"; and 10) "'The Pursuit of Happiness': The Crisis Caused by Debilitating Popular Culture." Hence, this first of these two volumes is entitled: *Born in Crisis*.

If naming these specific issues describes a situation somewhat similar to what we see happening all around us today, then you have a sense of what impelled me to embark on this literary journey. Then as now, these real life human crises continue to challenge and crush people. For this reason, Methodism's relevant story continues to challenge and encourage us, because it inspires us to try to find, as the early Methodists did, the spiritual strength and practical solutions to help alleviate these problems. It reminds us that we cannot live like Dives, who ignored and stepped over the broken man named Lazarus who lay at his gate each and every day (Luke 16:19–31). And that, as followers of Jesus Christ, we dare not see a person harmed or in trouble—whether or not they are of our race, religion, gender, or nation— and simply cross over to the other side of the road to avoid sharing in their plight, like the pious people of another one of Jesus' parables. Pious avoidance is not the norm for our Methodist heritage and story, and it is not the route we are called to take today. Methodists are called, instead, to live their lives by three simple rules: Do no harm. Do all the good you can. And to embrace spiritual attitudes and practices that help us stay in love with God.[2]

---

2. See early Methodism's historic "General Rules," in J. Wesley, *Works*, VIII, 270–71, or Job, *Three Simple Rules*. A study guide for small groups by Jeanne Torrence Finley *Three Simple Rules for Christian Living*, is also available.

Tragically, the Methodist family has also gone through significant internal strife, dysfunction, and trauma. Eight major theological, ecclesial, and ethical controversies tried the Methodist's values, tested their patience, strained familial relationships, and sometimes divided their family. These have led to a few institutional marriages, and more than a few divorces stemming from matters like: 1) disagreement about the nature of Christian spiritual life, faith, and good works; 2) controversy over predestination and the comfort of Christian salvation; 3) the difficulties associated with living out Christian Perfection in an imperfect world; 4) the pain and trauma of ecclesiastical separation; 5) controversy over the validity of women's leadership; 6) the debilitating effects of racism and racial segregation; 7) controversy over institutional governance and shared leadership; and 8) disagreement over the affirmation and full inclusion of LGBTQI people. These specific controversies and disagreements within "the family" have challenged, pained, and changed Methodism. They are examined in volume 2 of this set, *Shaped by Controversy*.

CHAPTER 1

"Don't Let Them Pull the Wool over Your Eyes"

The Crisis of Mixing Religion and Politics

THE SOCIAL FABRIC OF eighteenth-century England was profoundly shaped by the "establishment" status of the Church of England (COE) as the realm's only legal church. The Church was born in the sixteenth-century Reformation when Henry Tudor, King Henry VIII, wrestled control of the Christian (at that time Roman Catholic) Church from the pope in Rome and consolidated both church and state under his authority. This transition was achieved through a series of Parliamentary Acts and Royal Decrees, epitomized by the Act of Royal Supremacy (1534), which made Henry and his heirs "the supreme head of the Church in England."

The Act of Royal Supremacy further stipulated that "his heirs and successors, kings of this realm, shall have full power and authority from time to time to visit, repress, redress, record, order, correct, restrain, and amend all such errors, heresies, abuses, offenses, contempts and enormities, whatsoever they be, which by any manner of spiritual authority or jurisdiction."[1] Led by the monarch and supported by both tithes and taxes, the Church's "establishment" posture was true in a double sense; for nearly a century, it was the only legal Church in the realm, and the Church used its authority to buttress the sociopolitical *status quo*—"the establishment."

This arrangement broke down what was left of the medieval wall between the "religious life" of clerics, monks, and nuns, and the "secular"

---

1. Ross, "Henry VIII's 1534 Act of Supremacy," lines 8–9.

authority of kings and queens in England. Clergy sometimes held political office, even that of "first minister," and strategic seats in the upper house of Parliament, the House of Lords. It could be said that church and state had a "one hand washes the other" sort of relationship, which in theory built a better and more stable society. Indeed, that vivid description of mutual benefit through cooperation was also born in the same Tudor England that developed the religious establishment.[2] And although provisions where installed for "dissenters" to stand apart from the COE through the Toleration Act of 1689, in practice it meant that church and state were aligned in ways that protected the privilege of both political and religious leaders, often at the expense of people less fortunate than themselves.

One small example of the debilitating effects of the Church-state alliance were the "burial in woolen acts," which were established in the 1640s and lasted, in various forms, until 1814. They stipulated that any person who wished to be buried in Anglican "holy ground" had to be buried in "a shroud, shirt, or shift made entirely of wool." The family of the deceased was required to present a signed affidavit to the parish priest swearing conformity to this law prior to the interment of decedent with a "proper" church funeral and burial.

Burial in Wool Affidavit for John Winne, Merchant, of the Parish of St. Augustine, Bristol, **June 23, 1736, photograph by Heather Wolfe, Folger Shakespeare Library, Washington, DC. Folger MS Y.d.1794. Used with permission.**

2. The saying was first found in William Bavand's *Tochygne the Good Orderyne* (1599), which was a translation of an earlier German work. Bavand wrote: "As it were one hande washeth an other, one man aideth an other."

I have seen hundreds of these affidavits in local parish church records. Of course, a fee was also associated with swearing one out, and with a violation of the Act came a fine. If a woolen garment was not attested, the deceased was either barred from the churchyard or (more often) the family was fined 5£, which was roughly a week's wages for a working person.

The Burial in Woolen Acts were a thinly veiled attempt by the House of Lords to use COE pastoral practices to support their personal and financial interests in the British wool industry. Hence, the landed gentry used the Church "to pull the wool over the eyes" of grieving families who wanted to see their relatives buried in "holy ground." By the middle of the eighteenth century, rebellious middle-class religious people, like John Bryom's relatives, violated the act and proudly paid the fine as an act of protest against an unjust law.[3] The phrase, "Don't let them pull the wool over your eyes," was a protest as well as a bit of dark humor about the way the state-church alliance exploited pious poor people—even in death.

In 1689, Parliament's Act of Toleration granted non-Anglican Protestants who "dissented" from the Church's doctrine or practice a degree of religious freedom. But the COE retained its "most favored" status under law, and this impacted society and religion in many ways. For example, the Test Act (1673) required that anyone seeking public office had to be a member and communicant in the COE. Similar requirements were also in place for entrance into the universities and military. In the eighteenth century, voting in parliamentary elections was limited to men over twenty-one who owned land worth forty shillings, and who were not Roman Catholics or Jews. Because of these restrictions, in 1780, for example, the voting electorate amounted to only 214,000 people out of a population of almost 8 million, or about 3 percent of the populace.[4] Just as there were religious tests (either explicit or implicit) for advancement in civil life, political pull or "preferment" was often needed for ecclesiastical appointment or promotion.

Ecclesiastical preferment, too, often became a way of rewarding political favors or making powerful and influential friends within the establishment.[5] Sir Charles Petrie, a modern expert on the period, painted a dismal picture of ecclesial cronyism:

> The Church of England was at its nadir during the reigns of the first two Georges, and during the early years of George III. Convocation remained silenced, and ecclesiastical preferments, invariably made to serve political ends, were regarded by clergy

3. Whiteley, *Wesley's England*, 108.

4. See "Getting the Vote," para. 1.

5. See Sykes, *Church and State in England*, 147–88.

and laity alike as little more than desirable offices. Bishoprics
and deaneries were solicited from the Prime Minister of the day
with unblushing importunity.[6]

Or as the famous author Dr. Samuel Johnson (1709–84) lamented to his
friend, James Boswell: "No man can now be made a Bishop for his learning and piety, his only chance for promotion is his being connected with
somebody who has parliamentary interest."[7] A second deleterious result of
the Church-state alliance was that religion became a political issue. Theological heresy was synonymous with political treason, and as the nation's
religious pendulum swung dangerously towards Protestantism and then to
Catholicism and back to Protestantism again, pious people suffered and pious people died.

Queen Elizabeth's (1558–1603) "settlement" was a tacit compromise
that gave England a Church that *looked* Catholic in its liturgy, rites, Book of
Common Prayer, and vestments, and *sounded* Protestant in its attention to
the vernacular English Bible and the Thirty-Nine Articles of Religion. The
settlement sought to put an end to the war between the two sixteenth-century faiths based on the *outward* conformity of all her subjects, required by
Elizabeth's Act of Uniformity (1559), as well as the queen's willingness "not
to open windows into men's souls."[8] Since Elizabeth's "middle way" required
compromises on the part of Catholics and Protestants alike, extremists from
both groups wound up being oppressed, imprisoned, and driven from the
kingdom. The devout Catholics fled or closeted themselves in rural estates.
Radical Protestants, like the Puritans, who wanted to "purify" the COE of
the all the remnants of "popery" in favor of the plain worship and theology
of John Calvin, agitated for change and waited for an opportunity to seize
power.

Simmering beneath the apparent calm of the Elizabethan Settlement
were religious tensions that would eventually lead to civil war, revolution,
and several attempted invasions over the next 200 years. In 1649, the situation came to a head after five years of civil war. The "head" in question
belonged to England's Anglo-Catholic monarch, Charles I, who was executed for treason. After eleven grim years of staunchly Protestant Puritan
rule, Parliament restored the monarchy in 1660 with constitutional limitations as both Church and state mounted reprisals against Puritanism. In
the restoration, Anglo-Catholic worship was back in favor along with an

---

6. Petrie, *Four Georges*, 235.

7. Boswell, *Life of Samuel Johnson*, 528.

8. Black, *Reign of Queen Elizabeth*, 19.

anti-Calvinistic (Arminian) theology. Many "dissenters" refused to accept the liturgies and rubrics of the Book of Common Prayer and were persecuted for it.

Daniel Defoe (1660–1731), author of *Robinson Crusoe* (1719), was also a satirist and closeted religious dissenter. In 1702, he wrote an anonymously published pamphlet, entitled *The Shortest Way with the Dissenters or Proposals for the Establishment of the Church*. Writing as though he were a rabidly loyal Tory, Defoe pretended to defend the COE and the Crown from criticisms of the blood-thirsty Dissenters (Presbyterian and Congregationalists), who only fifty years before had toppled the monarchy. Defoe told the Dissenters, "The time for mercy is past, your day of grace is over, you should have practiced peace and moderation, and charity, if you expected any yourselves."[9] He cynically urged the establishment to make short work ("the Shortest Way") of the opposition: "How can we answer to God, to the Church, and to our posterity, to leave them entangled with fanaticism, error, and obstinacy, in the bowels of the nation; that in time may involve an enemy in the same crimes and endanger the utter extirpation of religion in the nation?"[10] The best answer to this dilemma was also the most obvious one: get rid of them. "I am not supposing that all the Dissenters in England should be hanged or banished," he wrote, "but . . . if a few of the ringleaders suffer, the multitude are dismissed, so a few obstinate people being made examples there's no doubt but the severity of the law find a stop in the compliance of the multitude."[11] Likening the Church of England to the crucified Christ, Defoe closed his treatise with a call to action:

> Alas the Church of England! What with Popery on the one hand and schismataicks on the other, how has she been crucified between two thieves. Now let us crucify the thieves. Let her foundations be established upon the destruction of her enemies . . . And may the God of truth put it into the hearts of all friends of truth, to lift up a standard against pride and antichrist, that the posterity of the sons of error may be rooted out from the face of this land forever![12]

Defoe's *The Shortest Way* met with mixed reviews. To some in the Anglican establishment, his feigned political extremism resonated with their own supremacist views quite well, while others recognized that in his exaggerations Defoe wrote with sarcastic invective. When it was discovered

9. Defoe, *Shortest Way*, 3.
10. Defoe, *Shortest Way*, 28.
11. Defoe, *Shortest Way*, 23.
12. Defoe, *Shortest Way*, 28–29.

he was mimicking the opinions of prominent Anglican clergy, his veil of anonymous authorship was pierced and Defoe was brought to trial for libel. He was found guilty and sentenced to three days of abuse in the public pillory, followed by residence in Newgate Prison until his sizable fine was paid. While he was imprisoned, Defoe lost his business, a brickworks, and with it the ability to pay his own fine. By the end of the year, however, his fine was mysteriously paid by a secret government source, and he atoned for his literary indiscretion by publishing a newspaper that presented a more favorable picture of the Anglican Church and her clergy. Defoe's religious satire, written with a political edge, resulted in his trial (fortunately *not* for treason), public shaming in the stocks, and a lengthy imprisonment that cost him his livelihood, entirely due to the Church-state alliance.

At the turn of the eighteenth century, the Kingdom of England experienced still another religious-political crisis as the English Tudor dynasty that had ruled the previous century died out. The most obvious though distant line of succession ran through their cousins, the Stuarts of Scotland. But anti-Catholic feelings and fears ran so deeply in Anglican England that Parliament turned to Protestant Duke George Hanover of Germany, the fifty-second person in the line of succession, to ascend to the British throne. King George I reigned from 1714–27 and made little or no attempt to learn English or the customs of his new subjects. Unsurprisingly, he was not popular. Both Roman Catholics and staunch English monarchists conspired to remove him in favor of Charles Edward Stuart (1720–88), a "pretender" for the throne from the Stuart line, "Bonnie Prince Charlie" of Scotland. The conspirators were called "Jacobites," and they mounted armed uprisings in 1715 and 1719, as well as invasions of England in 1744 and again in 1759. Witty lines offered by John Byrom (1692–1773) reflected the feelings of the many who felt that German George of Hanover, "the Defender of the Faith," was every bit the "pretender" at being the King of England that Bonnie Prince Charlie was:

> God bless the King. I mean our Faith's Defender,
> God bless—no harm in blessing—the Pretender;
> But who Pretender is or who is King,
> God bless us all; that's quite another thing.[13]

Susanna Annelesy Wesley (1669–1742), the mother of John and Charles, harbored Jacobite sentiments, as did a number of the Wesleys' close friends. Reginal Ward suggested that Susanna's ambivalence about the current government continued in her sons: "[John] Wesley . . . was born of the

13. Byrom, *Private Journal and Literary Remains*, II:122.

Jacobite issue, and born into a rabidly Tory circle which damned foreigners, foreign religions, and foreign entanglements, kept up Jacobite sentiment far down the eighteenth century."[14] In this politically charged climate, those who drew large crowds and criticized either the Church or government, like John and Charles Wesley did with their evangelism *alfresco,* fell under suspicion and special scrutiny.

Critics of the Church of England were often seen as religious heretics as well as political traitors because of the way Church and state walked hand in hand. For example, a "harmless ditty" sung around Cornwall reported: "Charley Wesley is come to town, To try if he can pull the churches down."[15] While the Methodists consistently presented themselves as trying to reform the Church from within, the anonymous author of *The Methodists, an Humorous Burlesque Poem* (1739) believed he/she saw an opposite effect:

> They *with the* Church establish'd *join,*
> Its Pow'r the more *to undermine.*
> By Rule they eat, by Rule they drink,
> Do all things else by Rule but think.
> Accuse their *Priests* of loose Behavior,
> To get more in the Laymen's Favor,
> *Method* alone must guide 'em all,
> Whence METHODISTS, themselves, they call,
> Here I [Satan] my Triumphs fix to come,
> And here shall thou fix thine, O *Rome!*[16]

It was widely rumored that the Methodists prayed for the Roman Catholic "pretender" in their clandestine meetings, and on least one occasion, March 15, 1744, Charles Wesley was forced to appear before a justice of the peace because a warrant was issued against him for having spoken "some treasonable words."[17] Since treason was one of the many offenses that carried the death penalty in eighteenth-century England, this charge had potentially dangerous consequences, even though it was based on a misunderstanding of Charles's words. A month later, John Wesley met a Methodist society that had been victimized by mob violence because of rumors that Wesley helped Charles Stuart enter England disguised as one of his traveling preachers, John Nance.[18] With stories like these circulating about them, it is small wonder that the Wesleys and their Methodists were attacked by angry

14. Ward, *Protestant Evangelical Awakening,* 300.
15. J. Wesley, *Journal and Diaries* II:335.
16. Lyles, *Methodism Mocked,* 152. Emphasis original.
17. C. Wesley, *Manuscript Journal* II:395–400.
18. J. Wesley, *Journal and Diaries* III:22.

mobs.[19] At least one early Methodist preacher, William Seward (1711–70), died as a result of mob violence.[20]

Because they were viewed as traitors to Church and state, Methodists and their traveling preachers rarely received legal protection from local authorities; representatives of Church and state were more apt to instigate violence against them than to stop it. John Walsh noted,

> Many of those who took part in the mobbings were moved by ideas as well as irrational drives . . . [which they] justified in terms of social necessity or religious duty. There were villagers who felt that the Church Militant had the right to use a certain amount of deterrent force against those who threatened it, and: "prove their doctrine orthodox by apostolic blows and knocks."[21]

John Wesley remembered that the justice of the peace of Otley, near Leeds, addressed a large anti-Methodist mob by saying: "Do what you will to them just so you break no bones."[22]

The Methodist critique of the gentry of both Church and state rarely won the Methodists friends in high places; Anthony Steele remembered seeing a nobleman of Middleton, Yorkshire, pick up a club and join a mob while "swearing most dreadfully that the Methodists should not take his land from him."[23] The intrusion of Methodist traveling preachers into established Anglican parishes raised resentment against them among Church leaders, and their criticism of local clergy brought vocal opposition and sometimes violence. Lay preacher John Nelson, who was beaten and left for dead by angry mobs near Ackham, remembered: "The parson's brother cursed me, and said, 'According to your preaching, you would prove our ministers to be blind guides and false prophets; but we will kill you as fast as you come.' One said, 'If Wesley come on Tuesday, he shall not live another day in this world.'"[24] These did not seem like idle threats, given the example of William Seward, who was murdered by a mob at "the Hay," in Wales, on October 22, 1740.[25]

---

19. Cf. Rack, *Reasonable Enthusiast*, 270–82; Wilder, *Methodist Riots*; J. Walsh, "Methodism and the Mob."

20. Heitzenrater, *Wesley and the People Called Methodists*, 127.

21. J. Walsh, "Methodism and the Mob," 213–22.

22. J. Wesley, *Journal and Diaries*, IV:21.334.

23. Steele, *History of Methodism*, 218, cited by J. Walsh, "Methodism and the Mob," 218.

24. T. Jackson, *Lives of Early Methodist Preachers*, 1:162.

25. J. Wesley, *Journals and Diaries*, II:19.172.

Under the restored constitutional monarchy and the initial ineptitude of the Hanover dynasty, Parliament and the prime minister took an increasingly larger role in the governance of the nation. Two main political parties—Whigs and Torys, who held almost opposite views—vied for power. William Thomas Morgan opened a window into the polarized politics of the era as he described the parliamentary election of 1710:

> This election was at once a contest between the landed gentry and the moneyed men; between the supporters of the Hanoverians and the Stuarts; a test for the prerogative and the doctrine of passive obedience; a conflict between the High Church on the one hand and the Low Church and Dissenters on the other.[26]

London, which was a Tory political stronghold, became a political powderkeg when the Whigs gained ground in a series of parliamentary elections. In the summer of 1716, three regiments of British troops were billeted on Hyde Park Green just to keep the peace.[27] The Tories controlled the House of Lords, while the Whigs dominated in the House of Commons during much of the Georgian period, which led as easily to political conflict as it did to stalemate.

Quite a lot of ink has been spilled over trying to identify the political pedigree of John Wesley within this political mix.[28] He sounded very much like a Tory when he made statements like: "Above all, mark that man who talks of loving the Church and does not love the King. If he does not love the King, he cannot love God. And if he does not love God, he cannot love the Church."[29] John Wesley loved England's constitutional monarchy along with the Church of England, but he also critiqued both Church and state in ways that sounded very Whig-like. As a Christian moralist, John Wesley sought a balance point between his obligations of loyalty "to higher powers" (Rom 13) and the prophetically critical voice of Jesus and the great prophets of Israel. It might be said that Wesley's love and loyalty for the Church and state were precisely what fueled his critique of a few particular policies and caused him to speak out in favor of human rights and against hurtful and unjust situations of those around him.[30] Like a Tory, John Wesley supported the Crown during the "war of the American rebellion," which

---

26. Morgan, "Eighteenth-Century Election in England," 590.

27. Rogers, "Popular Protest in Early Hanoverian London," 70–81.

28. Vickers, *Wesley*, 60–82, offers a comprehensive discussion of the pertinent literature.

29. J. Wesley, *Works*, XI:196.

30. Vickers, *Wesley*, 72–73.

was characterized as a long, draining, and unwinnable war:[31] an eighteenth-century version of the war in Vietnam or Afghanistan.[32] But, like a Whig, he advocated for the natural rights and liberty of all humans.[33] Ever the conscientious citizen, Wesley's "Advice to a Freeholder" was to use his vote with prayerful discernment rather than sell it or trade it for a meal or a stiff drink, no matter how needful or enticing those alternatives to an honest vote may have been.[34]

Their utter loyalty to both Church and state provided the context within which the Methodists sometimes opposed particular governmental policies and practices as being unjust, immoral, or harmful. John Wesley was a critic of the enclosure laws and governmental policies that fenced off public lands and ultimately forced "small holders" from their lands while favoring the large "monopoly farms" of the gentry—and he was right; by the year 1800, more than 180,000 small farms disappeared.[35] Wesley argued that soaring national debt was destroying Britain's economy, as well as the liveli-hoods of many good people, because it created an impossible tax burden.[36] When he made up a list of "National Sins and Miseries," British colonialism did not escape his critique.[37] The Wesleys attacked the triangle trade's chat-tel slavery in sermon, song, and pamphlets as "the sum of all villainies." They decried it as a sin against God and the humanity of people of African descent.[38] Wesley and the Methodists tacitly combined elements of con-temporary political views and subsumed them within the larger project of Methodism's stated mission: "to reform the nation, particularly the Church; and to spread scriptural holiness over the land."[39]

In response to political crisis, the Wesleys advocated both patient loyalty and constructive criticism. They preached a gospel of personal and social transformation that was actualized in the life of the Church and in Methodist small groups (classes and bands), where they created a

---

31. While the war of the American Rebellion was winnable for the Kingdom of Great Britain up through 1777, the critics of Prime Minister, Lord North (1770–82), consistently characterized the war as "unwinnable" thereafter. See, for example, Ferling, "Myths of the American Revolution."

32. J. Wesley, *Works*, XI:80–90.

33. J. Wesley, *Works*, XI:34–46.

34. J. Wesley, *Works*, XI:196.

35. Whiteley, *Wesley's England*, 33.

36. J. Wesley, *Works*, XI:55–58.

37. J. Wesley, *Sermons*, III:574.

38. J. Wesley, *Works*, XI:59–79.

39. J. Wesley, *Works*, VIII:299.

counterculture of equity, up-lift, and generosity by practicing a spirituality that was easily summarized by their "three simple rules":

> [By] doing no harm, by avoiding evil in every kind; especially that which is most commonly practiced . . . [by] doing good of every possible sort, as far as possible, to all men; to their bodies . . . [and] to their souls . . . Thirdly, by attending upon all the ordinances of God . . . the ministry of the world, either read or expounded; the supper of the Lord; family and private prayer; searching the Scriptures; and fasting or abstinence.[40]

Their spirituality produced an outlook on life that was not "all about the money." For the early Methodists, "Christian stewardship" meant living one's entire life with gratitude and humility for what God has given, enjoying and employing our whole selves to service to our whole world—"all thy heart, all thy mind, and all thy soul; and love thy neighbor as thyself" (Matt 22:36–40). Their advocacy for gratitude, generosity, and their preference for simplicity put the Methodists on a collision course with the unbridled consumption and profit-taking that came with the eighteenth-century alliance between Church, political power, and the beginnings of industrialization. They sought, as Jesus said, to "Render therefore unto Caesar the things which are Caesar's; and unto God the things that are God's" (Matt 22:21). But their world also needed changing, and so the Methodists tried to "be not conformed to this world: but be ye transformed by the renewing of your mind, that ye may prove what is that good, and acceptable, and perfect, will of God" (Rom 12:2). This was (is) a path that required constant discernment and accountability to sort out which are "the things which are of Caesar" and "the things that are God's." It was/is a call and holy vocation to be a transformed transformer that requires deep draughts of God's grace as well as our own holy creativity.

QUESTIONS FOR FURTHER CONSIDERATION:

1. What forces bring us to political and religious polarization? How can these be overcome?

2. What is the church's role *vis-à-vis* political authority? What are the challenges (or trade-offs made) you see in being a good citizen as well as a person of faith?

40. J. Wesley, *Works*, VIII:270–71.

3. How do you balance political loyalty along with making constructive political contributions with faith-based critique and responsible dissent?

4. Do you see instances of the ill effects of religious and/or political polarization at work today? Where? Why? What to do?

5. To what extent do political policies and economic pressures shape your individual life and the lives of others—both in positive and negative ways?

CHAPTER 2

"A Reasonable Enthusiast"[1]

The Challenge of Being a Person of Faith in the Age of Reason

J. M. Williams, *John Wesley*, **c. 1743, oil on canvas, 89 x 66.5 cm, Oxford Center for Methodism and Church History, Oxford Brooks, Oxford. Used with permission.**

1. The phrase "reasonable enthusiast" is from Rack, *Reasonable Enthusiast*, xii, who in turn borrowed it from Wesley's critic, Alexander Knox. Rack's reminder of the need to "penetrate the Wesley legend created by his followers and biographers and the smoke-screen created by Wesley himself" in order to understand the paradoxes of his "enigmatic personality" bears repetition.

13

THE WORLD IN WHICH Methodism was born was a product of the Age of Reason. John Locke (1632–1704), whom John Wesley described as "that great master of reason,"[2] and the Wesley brothers were contemporaries. Locke's *Essay Concerning Human Understanding* (1690) set the intellectual tone of the day. John Wesley read the essay with appreciation, because Locke's emphasis on a common-sense approach to reason echoed his own desire to "mark down a middle way" between "those extremes, overvaluing and undervaluing reason."[3] Wesley's admiration for Lockean common sense and a middle way resonated with his own temperament as well as his Anglican religious roots. It was voiced in statements like: "We talk common sense . . . both in verse and prose,"[4] and was given extended treatment in Wesley's *An Earnest Appeal to Men of Religion and Reason* (1743), and *A Farther Appeal to Men of Reason and Religion* (1745).

The John Wesley of the *Appeals* was also the "strangely warmed" enthusiast that makes up the other side of Henry Rack's paradoxical description of him as "the Reasonable Enthusiast." "Enthusiasm" was a negative term in eighteenth-century religious parlance; rather than describing excitement, zeal, or ardor, enthusiasm was a synonym for religious fanaticism. The poet John Dryden (1631–1700), who lived through the horrors of the English Civil War, associated enthusiasm with the "God told me so" sort of divine certainty with which the Puritans embraced their violent revolution: "A numerous host of dreaming saints succeed,/Of the true old Enthusiastic breed;/'Gainst form and order they their pow'r employ/Nothing to build, and all things to destroy."[5] Locke's *Essay* also reflected a negative connotation for enthusiasts, since it described people who attributed to God ideas that are not accountable to reason: "Their minds being thus prepared," he wrote, "whatever groundless opinion comes to settle itself upon their fancies, is an illumination from the Spirit of God."[6] Dr. Samuel Johnson's famous *Dictionary* (1755) defined enthusiasm as: "A vain belief of private revelation; a vain confidence of divine favor or communication."[7]

The Wesleys' contemporaries harbored these negative connotations for "enthusiasm" when they assessed them as well as their Methodism. Dr. Johnson's definition of enthusiasm lurked behind the words of Anglican

2. J. Wesley, *Sermons* II:589.

3. J. Wesley, *Sermons* II:588–89.

4. Hilderbrandt and Beckerlegge, "Preface," 7:74.

5. Dryden, "Absolom and Achitopel," lines 529–32.

6. Locke, *Essay Concerning Human Understanding*, II:432; see especially ch. 19, "On Enthusiasm," 438–41.

7. *Johnson's Dictionary of the English Language*, s.v. "enthusiasm."

Bishop Joseph Butler when, during a tense meeting with John Wesley in August 1739, Bishop Butler scolded Wesley: "Sir, the pretending to extraordinary revelations and gifts of the Holy Ghost is a horrid thing, a very horrid thing."[8] Wesley's reply was illuminating: "I pretend to no *extraordinary* revelations or gifts of the Holy Ghost—none but what every Christian may receive, and ought to expect and pray for."[9] But there was also enough irregularity to Wesley's spirituality, such as his practice of sometimes relying upon praying and casting lots to help make a difficult decision, to give some credence to his bishop's concerns. Bishop Butler was rightly concerned that Wesley's advocacy for religious experience might involve private, "hot-line-from-heaven" revelations that circumvented the reasonable boundaries provided by the Anglican "three-legged stool" of religious verification: Scripture, tradition, and reason.[10] By definition of the *New General English Dictionary* (1735), an "enthusiatical" person was guided by "wild, irregular, emotion belonging to or acted upon by the spirit of Enthusism, delusion or madness."[11] In the Age of Reason, an "enthusiast" was an irrational person, someone who was "crazy for God."

Hubert Francois Bourguignon, *Enthusiasm Display'd or the Moor-fields Congregation,* **1739, print, 214 x 287 mm, British Cartoon Prints Collection of the Library of Congress Prints and Photography Division, Washington, DC. LC.–USZ62–137507.**

8. J. Wesley, *Journal and Diaries* I:471.

9. J. Wesley, *Journal and Diaries* I:471. Emphasis original.

10. The "three-legged stool" stems from the works of Rev. Richard Hooker (1554–1600).

11. *New General English Dictionary,* s.v. "enthusiast."

A satirical cartoon, "Enthusiasm Display'd 0R the Moor-Fields Congrega-tion" (1739), by C. Corbett, illustrated well the reputation the Methodists earned because of the emotional outbursts that often accompanied their evangelism. The cartoon depicted the properly wigged young preacher levi-tating in the air, wildly gesturing over a clutch of swooning women. They seem to be smitten by the Spirit, but since they are also drinking heavily, they may have passed out because of the spirits instead. Each woman carries a theatrical mask, with which she is "two-faced" and well equipped to hide her true self. The cartoon depicts a gentleman, wearing a three-cornered hat, standing in the right rear of the crowd. Wearing a curiously bemused smile, he represents reason's vantage point amidst a crowd of enthusiasts. To the reasonable gent, the display looked more like cheap theatre than true religion. It was, in the minds of some, a short step from the "street theatre" of open-air evangelism to the satirical reproduction of the real thing. By 1739, plays like *The Mirror* and *The Mock-Preacher* lampooned Methodism on the London stage.[12] Critiquing the Methodists in sermon, songs, poems, and satires became so popular in Georgian England that Richard Green was able to discover the titles of 606 anti-Methodist publications.[13]

Despite the popular depictions, the Wesley brothers were no friends of enthusiasm. They disapproved of emotional outbursts and spiritual ex-tremism. The experience John Wesley defended in his conversation with Bishop Butler was the *Gefühl,* or "feeling" of God's acceptance, he learned from the German Moravians and personally experienced during a religious meeting on Aldersgate Street on May 24, 1738.[14] John told the bishop that he advocated for "no *extraordinary* revelations or gifts of the Holy Ghost," rather just the ordinary ones promised by the Scriptures, like Romans 8:16: "The Spirit itself beareth witness with our spirit, that we are the children of God." To that end, John Wesley published two "standard sermons" on the "witness of the Spirit"[15] describing the inner sense of God's acceptance that came with understanding oneself as a child of God.

Charles Wesley in particular had little patience for enthusiastic re-sponses to his preaching like screaming and shouting while being "smitten by the Spirit." He urged enthusiastic people to be still or be gone. And when a spirit-filled, enthusiastic disciple of the French Prophets tried to impress Charles by "speaking in tongues" (*glossolia*), he told the man he sounded more like a gobbling turkey than a prophet of God. Since Wesley couldn't

---

12. Lyles, *Methodism Mocked*, 165.

13. Lyles, *Methodism Mocked*, 15.

14. J. Wesley, *Journal and Diaries* I:242–52.

15. J. Wesley, *Sermons* I:267–99.

hear the voice of God in his colleagues' discourse, Charles offered to exorcise the prophet's demons.[16] John also disliked it when people "cried out so" during worship because of the distraction it caused for others, so he had them escorted out of the door.[17] But there was also enough irregularity to Wesley's spirituality to give some credence to Bishop Butler's concerns.[18] Ironically, thirty years later, John Wesley found himself taking on Bishop Butler's role as a gatekeeper when Wesley tried to rein in the rank enthusiasm of two of his leading lay preachers who became convinced they were "as perfect as angels" and could predict the soon-to-come end of the world.[19] The early Methodists' enthusiasm was generally tempered by a Lockean love for common sense, as well as Anglicanism's three-legged stool. But the Methodists also added a fourth leg, "experience," to the Anglican stool because of their concern for experiential religion in the face of deism.

The religious expression of the Age of Reason was deism, a rational and moralistic version of Christianity which had a marked preference for natural theology and a decided bias against miracles and the supernatural. Locke's *The Reasonableness of Christianity as Revealed in the Scriptures* (1695), for example, brought Christian faith under the penetrating scrutiny of reason. Because of deism's emphasis upon the physical world as opposed to the supernatural one, it was seen as an ally of emerging science when traditional Christianity too often seemed to be its opponent. Edward Hebert, Lord Cherbury (1583–1648), is considered the father of English deism; he was a renaissance man accomplished in many fields, including art, poetry, and philosophy. His *De Veritate* ("On the Truth," 1633) offered a five-point summary of his rational religion: (1) there is a Supreme Power—whom we may call God; (2) this Sovereign Power must be worshiped; (3) virtue (morality) combined with piety is the best part of divine worship; (4) all vices are hateful to God and should be expiated by repentance; and (5) there are rewards and punishments beyond this earthly life. His *De Religione Gentilium* ("The Religion of Gentiles," 1663) demonstrated that all the main world religions embraced these same five "truths."[20]

Under the intellectual impact of deism, eighteenth-century Anglican preaching took a decided turn towards an emphasis on conventional morality. While well-intentioned and necessary, given the age's moral decay, this shift seemed to turn popular preaching away from God's transforming grace.

16. C. Wesley, *Manuscript Journal* I:156.
17. J. Wesley, *Journal and Diaries* II:126.
18. This will be discussed in chapter 13.
19. This event will be discussed more fully in chapter 3.
20. *Encyclopedia Britannica Online*, s.v. "Edward Herbert, First Baron."

What people too often heard was a graceless, arithemetic piety that turned the Christian gospel into a balance sheet for salvation as each person hoped that they could count up more good deeds than bad ones. While stressing a needed moral message, this kind of preaching too often degenerated into works-righteousness, in which one's good deeds here were rewarded with eternal life in the world to come. Ironically, all the moralistic preaching of the Georgian age did not seem to lead to increased moral living; in fact, quite the opposite was true.

Since the deism lacked a stress upon divine grace and a robust Christology, it also lacked the power to transform, beyond the sheer force of human will and determination. Regrettably, lewd and antisocial behavior increased, perhaps because to the poor this approach seemed to say: "You will never make it." Spiritual hopelessness often sapped their moral energy—"Why bother?" it seemed to say. The age of John Locke was also the age of Adam Smith (1723–90), the father of modern capitalism. Emergent capitalism and *The Wealth of Nations* (1776) soon replaced religion as another and more tangible way for persons to assure themselves that their lives were successful; capitalism and financial success offered comfort in tangible ways that religion could not. But material certainty was far out of the reach of many people, especially the poor or otherwise disadvantaged. So there was a feeling of futility attached to many people's lives, and when organized religion failed to address it, people of all social ranks began to consider religion to be irrelevant, albeit for different reasons.

While pious deists and many others worked hard to keep salvation's balance sheet more full of good deeds than bad, emergent capitalists and materialists clung to their financial success or luxurious goods as a tangible signs of God's favor. The enthusiastic Methodists looked to the fact of classical Christian doctrines which were verified within themselves by listening for the confirming voice of God's Spirit. The Spirit whispers words of God's great love and acceptance to the human heart, "whereby we cry, 'Abba, Father'" (Rom 8:15). In the *Abba* experience, a Christian believer receives a profound sense of being a child of God, "heirs of God, and joint-heirs with Christ" (Rom 8:17), which is verified by the "love of God shed abroad" in human hearts.[21] They receive through the witness of the Spirit a sense of God's acceptance, a feeling of being at home with God.

The Wesleys and their Methodists sought a middle way between the extremes of enshrining reason on the one hand, and eschewing it on the other. This allowed them to retain the supernaturalism of classical Christianity

---

21. These phrases, based on Galatians 5:22, and Romans 5:5, became Wesleyan catchphrases for describing "Witness of the Spirit" (Rom 6:16–17).

founded in Jesus Christ—very God and very man. Because of their belief that Christ brought God's transforming grace into the lives of women and men everywhere, their message was one of optimism and change. It was also seen in their willingness, as John Wesley put it, "to plunder the Egyptians" (Exod 3:22); that is, to borrow and repurpose whatever ideas or practices communicated God's truth, irrespective of their original source.[22] Methodism's famous fourfold approach to religious knowledge is a good example of its eclectic theological mood, since it was, essentially, the Anglican three-legged stool, plus one. The primacy of the Bible rests in its identity as the written word of God that reveals God's living Word, Jesus Christ, our Lord. Tradition, reason, and experiences are resources that help us understand, interpret, and apply the teachings of Scripture to our lives. The concept of fourfold sources lives on in the ordination questions of the United Methodist Church and several other churches in the Wesleyan tradition.[23]

The Age of Reason also taught the Methodists of the rational difficulty of some basic Christian beliefs, like the doctrine of the Holy Trinity. John Wesley affirmed his belief in the Trinity based on the words of Scripture and the Anglican Articles of Religion. He considered the Trinity a watershed doctrine that distinguished authentic Christianity from the deism of his day, a belief which had to be a part of his life of faith. The "form," or the theological payload, of the doctrine of the Trinity was, in Wesley's view, a Christian belief of "deep importance."[24] But it was the theological content of the belief that was important; the affirmation of one God in three Persons.[25]

The manner of expressing one's belief in one God, in three Persons, or whether one even used words like "person" and "substance" or "Trinity" to describe that belief, was of no particular importance to Wesley.[26] Speaking like a child of the Age of Reason, John Wesley opined: "The Bible does not require you to believe any mystery at all. The Bible barely requires you to believe such *facts*, not the manner of them. Now the mystery does not lie in the *fact*, but altogether in the *manner*."[27] And to those who might scruple because they cannot explain the inner workings of the Trinity ("the *form* of the doctrine"), Wesley pointed out that common-sense reason allows a person to believe in many things that cannot be completely understood and

---

22. Outler, *Theology in the Wesleyan Spirit*, 1–23.

23. United Methodist Church, *Book of Discipline*, para. 330. There is an excellent discussion of the theological use and interaction of Scripture, tradition, reason, and experience in *Book of Discipline*, para. 105: "Our Theological Task."

24. J. Wesley, *Sermons* II:376.

25. J. Wesley, *Sermons* II:376.

26. J. Wesley, *Sermons* II:378.

27. J. Wesley, *Sermons* II:383. Emphasis original.

satisfactorily explained: "God said, 'Let there be light'; and there was light. I believe it: I believe the plain *fact*; there is not mystery at all in this. The mystery lies in the *manner* of it. But of this I believe nothing at all; nor does God require it of me."[28] In other words, one can easily and reasonably believe in "the fact" of the existence of "light" without being able to explain its inner workings. So also with the air, the earth, the human soul, our physical body, and so on. Wesley argued: "I believe just so much as God has revealed [i.e., the fact of the matter] and no more. But this, the *manner*, he has not revealed; therefore I believe nothing about it. But would it not be absurd in me to deny the *fact* because I do not understand the *manner*?"[29]

In their middle-way use of common-sense reason, the Wesleys coopted the intellectual energy of the Enlightenment without being enslaved by it. Their Lockean common sense was counterbalanced by an advocacy for a version of Christianity that was felt and lived, as well as believed and thought. They "plundered the Egyptians," and their eclectic approach allowed the Methodists to embrace classical Christian doctrines and experiences as well as the new scientific and medical discoveries erupting around them. It was not an accident that John Wesley, the practical theologian, wrote a textbook on homeopathic medicine called *The Primitive Physic: An Easy and Natural Method of Curing Most Diseases* (1747), or that he owned one of the few electrostatic generators in 1750s London. His electric generator still sits on the corner of John Wesley's desk in the Methodist City Road Chapel in London as a silent witness to Wesley's belief that, since God made it, electricity was a good and useful thing. Wesley's theology told him electricity was, like all of God's creation, "very *good*" (Gen 1:31; emphasis added); John Wesley, the experimental theologian, spent more than forty years trying to figure out exactly what electricity was good *for*.

QUESTIONS FOR FURTHER CONSIDERATION:

1. It is possible, or even desirable, to be "a reasonable enthusiast" in today's world? And to "plunder the Egyptians?" Why? Why not?

2. Do the attractions of "modernism," like reason, science, anti-supernaturalism, works righteousness, and materialism, impact Christian faith today? How? Why?

28. J. Wesley, *Sermons* II:384. Emphasis original.
29. J. Wesley, *Sermons* II:385. Emphasis original.

3. Why do some people of faith feel threatened by advances in science or medicine? Why do some Christians hold a very negative attitude towards technology?

4. Why is the arithmetic theology of salvation (adding up your good deeds, subtracting the bad ones) so seductive to us, and yet also so destructive to the authentic life of faith?

5. Is the love and acceptance of others and of God important to you? Where do you look for tangible signs of God's acceptance?

CHAPTER 3

"Awake Thou That Sleepest"

The Crisis of Ecclesiastical Slumber and Dysfunction

EIGHTEENTH-CENTURY ENGLAND UNDERSTOOD ITSELF as "a Christian nation" because roughly 94 percent of the population (in 1760) were "nominal Christians" who had been baptized into the Church of England.[1] Church attendance was assumed by both English law and custom, but Anglican literature of the period laments plummeting church attendance and shockingly low levels of participation. It was a situation distressingly parallel to what is seen in mainline churches today; as Ed Stetzer recently remarked about church attendance in the *Washington Post*, "While the sky isn't falling, the floor is dropping out."[2]

The religious climate of Georgian England was well critiqued by artist and social critic William Hogarth (1697–1764). His "The Sleeping Congregation" lampooned the lethargy of Anglican worship services as a near-sighted priest, ensconced in his high pulpit, read his sermon to a somnolent congregation. So intent is his concentration on the sermon text before him that the preacher does not notice his entire congregation has fallen sound asleep, while his lector's attention was diverted from reading the Scripture text to ogle the exposed bosom of the young woman dozing beside him (1762).

---

1. Field, "Counting Religion in England and Wales."
2. Stetzer, "If It Doesn't Stem Its Decline," para. 3.

William Hogarth, *The Sleeping Congregation,* **1762, ink engraving on paper, 26.2 x 20 cm, Royal Collection Trust, St. James Palace, London. Used with permission. © Her Majesty Queen Elizabeth II .**

As he stood before "the university at Oxford," assembled in St. Mary's Cathedral on April 4, 1742, Charles Wesley's premise coincided well with Hogarth's "The Sleeping Congregation."

William Gush, *Charles Wesley Preaching,* **c. 1750, oil on canvas, 423 x 463 cm. Digital reproduction made by Adam Sk-commonswiki.**

Wesley intended to rouse his listeners from their complacent spiritual slumber by borrowing the words of Ephesians 5:14, "Awake thou that sleepest, arise from the dead, and Christ shall give thee light." One of Jonathan Swift's poems, in which he suggested that the congregants might as well fashion their church pews into bedsteads because of all the sleeping they did in church, offered a similar picture:

> A bedstead of the antique mode,
> Compact of timber many a load,
> Such as our ancestors did use,
> Was metamorphos'd into pews;
> Which still their ancient nature keep
> By lodging folks dispos'd to sleep.[3]

It is not clear whether Charles Wesley's hearers received any intended divine light through his sermon "before the University," but we know it had some impact, albeit negative, because this was the last time Charles was invited to preach at St. Mary's.

Another William Hogarth print, "Credulity, Superstition, and Fanaticism" (1762), critiqued the more animated evangelical preachers. In his enthusiasm, the preacher has literally jumped right out from under his wig. In his right hand, he dangled the alternatives of good life or bad before the congregation, with a marionette of an angel in his right hand and one of a devil in his left. Six shriveled souls are nailed to the front of his pulpit like so many trophies of an earlier conquest. The young couple reclining in romantic involvement directly below his pulpit have confused holy love with the more carnal kind. Half of the congregation are either smitten by the spirit or they are sound asleep; the amateur choir is led in their chorus by the sound of a baying hound. The artist's assessment was clear: the high church, or low church, each in their own way, were utterly ineffective.

---

3. Swift, "Baucis and Philemon," lines 101–6.

William Hogarth, *Credulity, Superstition and Fanaticism,* **1762, print, 46.8 x 35 cm, Metropolitan Museum, New York.**

Several issues conspired to undermine organized religion in the English eighteenth century. One of them was the theological pluralism and cultural individualism engendered by the Age of Reason, which Daniel Defoe described as the religious perspective of *The True-Born Englishman*(1701):

> In their religion they are so uneven,
> That each man goes his own by-way to Heaven.
> Tenacious of mistakes to that degree
> That ev'ry man pursues it separately,
> And fancies none can find the way but he:
> So shy of one another they are grown,
> As if they strove to get to Heaven alone.[4]

The religious individualism reported by Defoe led directly to nominal participation in the life of the Church on the one hand, and to deism on the other. Historian Roy Porter reports:

> Many Georgians rarely went through a church porch between
> their christening and burial. Yet practically everyone, in his

4. Defoe, *True-Born English Man,"* II:102–8.

own fashion, had faith. Much of it was a fig leaf of Christianity covering a body of inherited magic and superstition, little more than Nature worship . . . But everyone had his own vision of a Creator, of a "place" in Heaven, and convictions of Good and Evil, reward and punishment.[5]

While a more positive picture of official religion in Georgian England can be found, our attention to Methodist reports on the subject necessarily skews the report.[6]

The Methodists pointed to two specific resources that epitomized the theological and spiritual decline of the Church they loved. The first was an anonymous devotional treatise entitled *The Whole Duty of Man: Laid Down in a Plain and Familiar Way, for the Use of all, But Especially the Meanest Reader* (1658). It was an extremely popular treatise that was widely read for two centuries. The title and premise of the little book came from Ecclesiastes 12:13, "Let us hear the conclusion of the whole matter: Fear God, and keep his commandments: for this is the whole duty of man." Its emphasis upon "duty" and "keep" fit well the moralistic spiritual tenor of the times. The "meanest reader" of the subtitle refers to low-born or common people. *The Whole Duty of Man* was a "popular" devotional handbook: "The only intent of this ensuing treatise," explained its author, "is to be a short and plain direction to the very meanest readers, to *behave* themselves so in this world that they may be happy for ever in the next."[7] Behavior mattered—a lot—since it earned eternal happiness.

Although John Wesley abridged the *Whole Duty* for inclusion in his voluminous *Christian Library*, he never mentioned it in his published writings and, given the popularity of the treatise, it is a stunning silence. George Whitefield's reaction was less subtle; he "detested" the book, probably for its emphasis upon redemption by good works instead of justification by faith in Christ. Whitefield ceremoniously burned a copy of *The Whole Duty* in public protest on at least one occasion. Nor would he have been pleased to read that the "first" of the several things that Christ came to do for us was "to make known to us the whole will of His Father; in the *performance* whereof we shall be sure to be accepted and rewarded by Him. And this was one great part of His business which He performed in those many sermons and precepts we find set down in the Gospel."[8] Where the Methodists stressed the redemptive and restorative role of Jesus Christ as the starting point of

---

5. Porter, *English Society*, 168.

6. Cf. Sykes, *Church and State in England*.

7. Allestree, *Whole Duty of Man*, 1. Emphasis added.

8. Allestree, *Whole Duty of Man*, ix. Emphasis added.

their soteriology, *The Whole Duty* stressed Jesus' role as the revealer and example of successfully doing God's moral will.[9]

The Methodists also criticized the sermons of the best-loved Anglican preachers of the previous generation, including Rev. Dr. John Tillotson (1630–94), who was Archbishop of Canterbury (1691–94). John Wesley ranked Tillotson among the Anglican theologians who read the Bible through the lens of natural religion (deism). This perspective was evidenced throughout Tillotson's sermons: "Nothing ought to be received as a revelation from God which plainly contradicts the principles of natural religion or overthrows the certainty of them."[10] The Bishop's description of the way to salvation also reflected the moralistic "do good, be good" theology of the age, whereby one worked oneself into a position to receive God's grace:

> . . . the great business of religion is, to make men truly good, and to teach them to live well, and if religion have not this effect it matters not of what church any man lifts and enters himself; for most certainly, a bad man can be saved in none; tho's a man know the right way to heaven never so well and be entered into it, yet if he will not walk therein, he shall never come thither . . . But if we will in good earnest apply ourselves to the practice of religion and the obedience of God's holy laws, his grace will never be wanting to us to so good a purpose.[11]

George Whitefield offered stinging rebuke of what he considered Tillotson's capitulation of the gospel of saving and transforming grace in favor of a theology of good works. The Archbishop's sermons were "such husks, fit only for carnal, unawakened, unbelieving reasoners to eat," he quipped. On another occasion, Whitefield mused that Tillotson knew no more about being a "true Christian than had Muhammad."[12] Gerald Cragg summarized well the impact of Tillotson's sermons upon eighteenth-century Anglicanism: "If the next age treated religion either as an exercise in logic or an invitation to be upright on the most advantageous terms it was because Tillotson had taught it the lesson."[13]

It was from this spiritual malaise that Charles Wesley sought to awaken the gownsmen of Oxford on that day in April 1742. He told his stunned listeners that they were so asleep that they did not realize that they were dead in their sins. They needed to shake off their drowsy neglect and take

9. Allestree, *Whole Duty of Man*, 9.

10. Tillotson, *Works*, II:33.

11. Tillotson, *Works*, II:56.

12. Schlenther, "Whitefield, George, 1714–1770," I:2981.

13. Cragg, *Reason and Authority in the Eighteenth Century*, 20.

stock of themselves and their spiritual state, to awaken to repentance, which in Wesleyan theology is "true self knowledge." They also needed to awaken from the nightmare that was their lives, to rediscover the dream God had planted in the hearts of all humans, "to have the life of God" within their souls.[14] "Awake, thou that sleepest, and arise from the dead,'" Wesley urged. "God calleth thee now by my mouth, and bids thee know thyself, thou fallen spirit, thy true state and only concern below . . . Judge thyself, and thou shalt not be judged by the Lord."[15] Charles's call for corporate repentance concluded with a plea for divine deliverance, as well as a prayerful pledge to go forward with God: "Help us, O God of our salvation, for the glory of thy name; O deliver us, and be merciful to our sins, for thy name's sake. And so will we not go back from thee: O let us live, and we shall call upon thy name. Turn us again, O Lord God of hosts, show the light of thy countenance, and we shall be whole."[16]

The absence of theological clarity on the nature of Christian salvation, John Wesley opined, had robbed the Church of the "power of godliness." Where the power is gone, the departure of the "form of godliness" is not far behind: "Outward religion may be where inward is not; but if there is none without, there can be none within."[17] The Church of England, as Wesley saw it, was decaying from the inside out. He was not alone in this assessment. The published memoirs of public figures like Horace Walpole (1717–97) and Lord Hervey (1696–1743) showed they were "extremely bitter about the corruption, pluralism, pride of prelacy, and etc., then existing in the National Church."[18] After a painful survey of contemporary declining religious practice and decaying moral lives, John Wesley turned evangelist and pleaded for spiritual renewal: "My brethren, my heart bleeds for you. O that you would at length take knowledge and understand that these are the words of truth and soberness! O that you knew, at least in this your day, the things that make for your peace!"[19]

Bishop Tillotson was considered a "latitudinarian," which in the seventeenth century described one who advocated religious toleration and an end to religious controversy by minimizing "the importance of doctrine and

14. J. Wesley, *Sermons* I:147.

15. J. Wesley, *Sermons* I:147.

16. J. Wesley, *Sermons* I:158.

17. J. Wesley, *Sermons* I:158.

18. Whiteley, *Wesley's England*, 294.

19. J. Wesley, *Works* VII:462. Horace Walpole was son of Prime Minister, Sir Robert Walpole, and Lord John Hervey was Keeper of the Privy Seal, and a close confidant of King George II.

forms of worship in the interests of 'reasonable-ness.'"[20] By the middle of the eighteenth century, however, "latitudinarian" took on more negative connotations, at least for some. John Wesley's *Dictionary* (1753) reported that a "latitudinarian" is "one who fancies all religions are saving," and one year later, Dr. Samuel Johnson described the latitudinarian as "one who departs from orthodoxy."[21] Harvey Hill pinpointed the nature of this shift when he described "latitudinarians" as those who were "excessively willing to compromise on important matters of Christian doctrine, worship, and polity."[22] Once again, John Wesley, "the reasonable enthusiast," seemed to want to simultaneously affirm and deny the religious latitudinarianism of the Age of Reason. He was drawn to its liberality of inclusion, its desire to avoid unnecessary and hurtful controversies over Christian doctrine and practice, and he tried to embrace its tolerant attitude towards those who disagreed. But when "latitudinarian" described a departure from theological orthodoxy, it became a label and approach he could not follow.

The tension between these tendencies towards toleration and orthodox theological boundaries was evident at various places in early Methodism, but perhaps nowhere more clearly than in John Wesley's concept of "the Catholic Spirit." Epitomized in his standard sermon, the Catholic Spirit was a plea for Christian fellowship and cooperation that was based in Christian love; the *agape* love of 1 Corinthians 13. Drilling down to a foundation that was deeper than denominational identity, theological uniformity, or agreement about church polity or liturgy, Wesley asked: "Though we can't think alike, may we not love alike? May we not be of one heart, though we are not of one opinion? Without all doubt we may. Herein all the children of God may unite, notwithstanding these smaller differences. These remaining as they are, they may forward one another in love and in good works."[23]

But John Wesley also recognized that "the Catholic Spirit" might become a religious blank check with respect to Christian doctrine, or a synonym for "anything goes" with respect to Christian practice; so he set about to distinguish the Catholic Spirit from latitudinarianism: "The catholic spirit is not *speculative latitudinarianism*," he explained. "It is not an indifference to all opinions. This is the spawn of hell, not the offspring of heaven. This unsettledness of thought, this being 'driven to and fro, and tossed about with every wind of doctrine' [Eph. 4:14] . . . A man of a truly catholic spirit has not now his religion to seek. He is fixed as the sun in his

---

20. *Episcopal Dictionary of the Church*, s.v. "latitudinarian."
21. Quoted in Griffin, *Latitudinarianism in the 17th Century of England*, 12.
22. Hill, "Law of Nature Revived," 169.
23. J. Wesley, *Sermons* II:82.

judgment concerning the main branches of Christian doctrine."[24] Nor is the "Catholic spirit . . . any kind of *practical latitudinarianism*. It is not indifference to public worship, or as to the outward manner of performing it . . . [The Catholic Spirit] is not indifference to all congregations."[25] There was a wide difference, in John Wesley's view, between a religious tolerance born of having no fixed theological opinions or ardent Christian practices, and one's striving for a religious tolerance that is grounded in Christian love: "His heart is enlarged toward all mankind . . . he embraces with strong and cordial affection neighbors and strangers, friends and enemies. This is catholic or universal love. And he that has this is of a catholic spirit. For love alone gives the title to this character—catholic love is a catholic spirit."[26]

Alongside the theological and spiritual malaise the Methodists claimed to see at work in the mainline Church was the equally dangerous dilemma of institutional dysfunction. "The Anglican Church," wrote Roy Porter, "was the nation's largest and wealthiest institution, spearheaded by twenty-six bishops, each occupying a cathedral in which deans, canons, and prebends officiated (the higher clergy numbered some 1,000 in all). Beneath these, there were some 10,000 parishes—the whole of England was emparshied."[27] But this huge and potentially impactful corporate enterprise was, in John Wesley's view, "a rope of sand" that lacked spiritual strength, unity, and cohesion.[28] In a misguided approach to tolerance, the Church seemed to have abandoned accountability at all levels. From the worldly conduct of its bishops and clergy, all the way down the administrative pyramid to the spiritual direction of its local parishioners, the Church seemed incapable or unwilling to practice the remedies that it's own *Discipline* prescribed.

Church attendance, for example, had become for some just one more opportunity to flaunt their wealth and status. For "moneyed worldlings," wrote Whiteley, "Even attendance at church was ceremonial; my lord had to be preceded by two or more footmen in livery and with powered hair, one carrying a foot-warmer, another food and wine, another a Bible."[29] Scenes like these were apt to set off a person of John Wesley's sensibilities on the one hand, and on the other make the poor and servant-class people feel awkward and unwelcome at church.

---

24. J. Wesley, *Sermons* II:92–93. Emphasis original.

25. J. Wesley, *Sermons* II:94–95. Emphasis original.

26. J. Wesley, *Sermons* II:94–95.

27. Porter, *English Society*, 172. The "glebe" is parish land which is set aside for farming and for producing income for the parish priest.

28. Cragg, *Appeals to Men of Reason and Religion*, 301.

29. Whiteley, *Wesley's England*, 77.

Many eighteenth-century sources bewailed shockingly low levels of Church attendance in Georgian England despite the fact that Church attendance was supported by both law and custom. There was also growing awareness that many people were using the 1689 Act of Toleration as a dodge to avoid church and religion altogether. This was the opinion of Rev. Robert South, who wrote in 1716 that "the vulgar and less knowing part of the nation do verily reckon this, as an Act for Toleration, has utterly cancelled all former obligations which did, or might lie upon them, to join with the Church in the public worship of God."[30] Prominent bishops lamented the fact that fewer than a third of the congregants of many parishes attended the Church of England or any other place "of Divine Worship."[31] When several parliamentary acts which penalized nonattendance proved unenforceable and were repealed, conscientious layman John Disney opined it was an utter scandal that in "a Christian country," the "Church is hardly so full as the taverns and ale-houses at the same time." Writing in 1710, Disney laid the blame at the feet of local church authorities, the churchwardens whose duty it was to report nonattendees to the local constables, as well the constables and magistrates whose duty it was to admonish, correct, and try them.[32] The Church-state alliance that helped sustain the Church was breaking down in the face of changing times and changing social sensibilities. It is also clear that roughly having 8 percent of its pious congregants exit the Church of England by registering as Dissenters represented a steady drain upon Anglican resources—both tangible and spiritual.[33]

Clerical absenteeism was nearly as large a problem for the Church of England as were the disappearing congregants, and those two absences were not unrelated. The poverty of many parish parsons was both legendary and true. In 1736, for example, 5,638 parishes were regarded as "poor" because their benefices (the funds paid for parish appointment) were valued at under £50 per annum, and therefore fell below the national poverty line.[34] Under these conditions, pastors often resorted to serving several parishes simultaneously (pluralism), or were absent from their parishes (absenteeism) in search of more income and a better life elsewhere. Porter reports: "Many parsons were non-resident and pluralist, having installed cut-price curates [substitutes] to perform their ministry (these got 'leavings' not 'livings').

---

30. South, *Twelve Sermons and Discourses*, 536.

31. Field, "Schilling for Queen Elizabeth," 225.

32. Disney, *Essay upon the Execution of the Laws Against Morality and Prophaneness*, quoted in Field, "Shilling for Queen Elizabeth," 225–26.

33. Field, "Eighteenth-Century Religious Statistics."

34. Taylor, "Church and State in England," 12.

About a quarter of parishes did not have a resident minister, and this situation worsened."[35] The undereducated and underpaid curates who filled the pulpits of many small parishes were euphemistically called "mean readers" because they merely read to the congregation from the Anglican *Book of Homilies* (1547), and they did not read very well. Whiteley notes that

> most sermons preached by the eighteenth-century rural divines were probably taken almost verbatim from printed collections. Many of these could be described as "mere moral essays" and embodied in "words of learned length and thundering sound." Sermons . . . would be tame and colorless, cold, and artificial, lest they should offend the squire's susceptibilities.[36]

Clerical absenteeism and pluralism had deleterious effects upon parish life, as well as church attendance. As Norman Sykes observes: "Within the Church the division between the privileged minority and the depressed majority was deep; and the gulf was widened by the agglomeration of pluralities upon the fortunate favorites whose feet were set securely on the ladder of preferment."[37]

Pluralism (simultaneously holding several parish livings) signaled an unbridled pursuit of wealth and greed which caused an erosion of public confidence in the Church. It too was lampooned in the popular art of the period. A political cartoon, "The Fat Pluralist and His Lean Curates" (c. 1733), for example, depicts an extremely corpulent Anglican priest, thought to be Dr. John Lynch, being hauled about in a chariot drawn by six gaunt curates. Joining the pluralist in the chariot are fatted pigs and poultry—implying a few more good meals lay in his future, while Lynch uses a devotional book entitled *Self Denial* as his backrest. The wheels are coming off the chariot (the Church) as it runs over a book of the Thirty-Nine Articles of the Church of England. Dr. Lynch exclaims: "The Church was made for me, and not I for the Church." Rev. John Lynch (1697–1750) was a notorious pluralist. As the son-in-law of Archbishop William Wake (1657–1733), he simultaneously held seven lucrative pastoral livings and chaplaincies. When Lynch's behavior came to public notice, both men were ridiculed for their ecclesiastical mismanagement and profiteering.

---

35. Porter, *English Society,* 172,
36. Whiteley, *Wesley's England,* 317.
37. Sykes, *Church and State in England,* 147.

The Fat Plauralist and His Lean Curates, c. 1772, ink sketching, 103 x 152 mm,
British Museum, London.

The eighteenth-century Church of England also faced a significant problem regarding ministerial deployment; it did not have enough churches, and the churches the Church of England had were often located in the wrong places. The parochial system of earlier, preindustrial England was strongest in the south and south-midlands, where a majority of the churches were located. With the gradual growth of industry, however, people fled the rural regions in search of better-paying jobs in the cities of the industrializing mid-lands. The location of many Anglican churches reflected more the rural past than the industrial present and the future. This observation was borne out by a survey made by Lord Stanhope at the end of the century, which discovered that over 4 million people "had not the means of attending the Church."[38] Stanhope's survey indicated that more than one-half of the entire population of England had no real means of attending church.[39] Because of the Church-state marriage, the bureaucratic process for building new churches was so cumbersome that of the fifty new church structures Parliament reluctantly agreed to erect in London in 1711, only ten were ever completed.[40] Even if every baptized Anglican communicant, who was required by law and custom to attend the Church, was to do so, there was no seat for them, or else their proper parish "place" was in the wrong geographic place.

38. Tyson, "Why Did John Wesley Fail?," 177.

39. Mahon, "Key Dates in Census." Estimated population demographics for 1780 were 7.5 million, and 8 million for 1790.

40. Porter, *English Society,* 175.

Other "intangibles," like pew rental, kept eighteenth-century people—even pious people—from attending the Church. The "horse stall" pews were often either rented or owned by the elite families. A confusing patchwork of parish customs that circumvented Anglican Church law allowed pew rental and put extra funds into the hands of churchwardens or the pastor. In some locations, churchwardens actually guarded the rented pews and removed nonpaying customers; sometimes pews were locked so they could not be misused during their owner's absence. By 1818, pew rental, which had been illegal since the sixteenth-century English Reformation, had become so prevalent that Parliament required there be at least some "free seats" in each newly constructed place of worship. If a person visited a church or could not afford to pay for a pew, they would sometimes sit in the "gallery" (a balcony sometimes reached by ladder) or stand quietly in the rear.[41] The situation felt far less than welcoming.

The Wesleys and their Methodists resented practices like pew rental as hurtful and exclusionary. Since the Methodist "Large Rules" required their attendance at Anglican worship and reception of the Lord's Supper, as members of a parish church, they were generally among those who sat in the gallery or stood in the rear. Their rough clothing, crude manners, and lack of decorum were often the object of ridicule. If they had come to Church directly from work on the farm, in the factory, or in the mine, their odor also received special comment. Even John Wesley is reputed to have judged the size of some of his audiences with his olfactories; "the room was so full it stank," he observed. The Methodists were also often quite conspicuous as they left the Church in mass, marching off to supplement their Anglican experience with fellowship in a Methodist Society Room or Preaching House. The Methodist assembly rooms had backless benches. Open-seating was an architectural statement of egalitarianism and thrift. It was a clear contrast to ecclesiastical arrangements elsewhere. In a similar way, early Methodist worship was a liturgically accessible service of sermon and congregational song that did not depend upon literacy or prayer books as a prerequisite to full participation.

It has long been a truism that "Methodists sing their theology." This was especially true in the early years when Charles's hymns provided the soundtrack for the Wesleyan revival. The Wesleyan hymns were, as John described the *Collection of Hymns for the Use of the People Called Methodists* (1780), "A little body of experimental and practical divinity."[42] Their hymn book was the Methodists' Book of Common Prayer, as well as a theological

---

41. Heales, *History and Law of Church Seats*, I:145–55; II:134–38.

42. Hilderbrandt and Beckerlegge, "Preface," VII:74.

primer in verse. In contrast to worship at the Church of England, with professional choirs and performance music, the Methodists stressed congregational song in an obvious preference for participation over musicality. Where the Anglican service was rooted in the Book of Common Prayer, which presupposed either literacy or a great familiarity with the service, most Methodists believed they prayed better with both their eyes and their books closed.

For all the notoriety and public ridicule generated by their open-air evangelism in market squares, fields, docks, mine heads, and factory fronts, the Methodists were "missional" in their willingness to try to go where the people were. The heart and soul of early Methodism was the network of small accountability groups: classes, and bands where Christian faith was "caught" as much as it was taught. The Methodist Societies were a place where corporate and private prayer were learned, where the word of God was preached, taught, and read, where spiritual disciplines and Christian fellowship were practiced; where the spiritual disciplines Methodists esteemed as "the means of grace" came to life. Christian community (*koinonia*) grew among them as members embraced "works of piety" and "works of mercy" and provided pastoral care for each other. They would not be, by John Wesley's design and hope, "the rope of sand" he observed in the established Church.

QUESTIONS FOR FURTHER CONSIDERATION:

1. What parallels and suggestions does this slice of Methodist history offer for your community of faith?

2. How can political and religious polarization, ecclesiastical lethargy and dysfunction, be addressed and overcome? How can it be managed productively?

3. What crises do you see the church facing today? What can/should you do to make a difference individually? Institutionally?

4. Would greater attention to the crises, instead of institutional survival, help the church answer questions about relevancy and sustainability? How?

5. What can you do to be more welcoming and inclusive in the way you and your community live out your Christian faith?

CHAPTER 4

"The Most Class-ridden Country
under the Sun"

The Crisis of Class and Privilege

WRITING IN 1941, GEORGE Orwell opined: "England is the most class-ridden country under the sun."[1] The class prejudice and privilege Orwell observed in his native land, however accurate it was in his own day, was certainly a characteristic of eighteenth-century England.[2] The class structure that supported the British Empire from within was often described as "the great chain of being" (Latin: *scala naturae*, "scale of nature"). Emanating from God and flowing down through the ranks of the created universe, it gave philosophical and theological rationale for the social hierarchy based on patriarchy and class privilege. This pattern reached back to medieval feudalism and was buttressed by sources as diverse as the monarchy, the philosophy of Aristotle, the theology of Thomas Aquinas, the Church of England and its theology, and popular culture. This social pyramid pattern was so deeply woven into the social fabric of Georgian England that those near or at the top of it were almost unaware of its existence and pervasive influence.

---

1. Orwell, *England, Your England*, 53.
2. McInerney, "Better Sort," 47–53.

Didacus (Diego) Valdes, *The Scale of Nature*, 1579, plate etching.

This "natural order" of things was assumed by even the progressive literature of the age, like Alexander Pope's (1688–1744) *Essay on Man* (1734). He wrote: "Order is Heav'n's first law; and this confest, some are, and must be, greater than the rest, more rich, more wise . . ."[3] This "order" fit very well with the political, social, and ecclesial structures of Georgian England. It was also evident in the predestined election of the Calvinists, the orderly rational world of deism, and the *Catechism of the Church of England*, which asked: "What is thy duty to thy neighbor?" "To honor and obey the Queen, and all that are put in authority under her; *to submit* to all my governors, teachers, spiritual pastors, and masters; *to order myself lowly and reverently to all my betters* . . . and to *do my duty* in that state of life, unto which it shall please God to call me."[4]

The immensely popular treatise *The Fable of the Bees or Private Vices— Public Benefits* (1714), by Bernard Mandeville, assumed that hierarchy and class distinctions were necessary for the all English worker "bees" to work

3. Pope, *Essay on Man*, IV:49–50.
4. Church of England, *Catechism*, Article X. Emphasis added.

well together in the well-ordered world of their hive. This concept was illustrated by George Cruikshank's British Bee Hive (1840).[5] Mandeville also
argued that "private vices," like selfishness, competition, and exploitation,
vices which were hypocritically decried by a "Christian nation," were actually the glue that held society together and produced (as his subtitle suggested) "public benefits." It both acknowledged and then justified the role
that "vices" like selfishness and exploitation had upon society because of
their "public benefit." Instead of pressing for the reform of society's vices
and ills, like privilege and paternalism, Mandeville's assessment supported
the *status quo*.

Many people, most particularly society's "betters," like the Anglican
theologian and member of Parliament Soame Jenyns (1704–87), saw social
harmony as one of the great benefits of the "one great Chain of Being." Jenys
likened social hierarchy to the proper order of an eighteenth-century English household:

> The universe resembles a large and well-regulated family in
> which all the officers and servants . . . are subservient to each
> other in a proper subordination; each enjoys the privileges and
> perquisites peculiar to his place, and at the same time contrib-
> utes, by that just subordination, to the magnificence and happi-
> ness of the whole.[6]

Social equality seemed, to Jenys, to be an irrational affront to God and the
divine order of things: "A government composed of all Kings, an army of all
Generals, or a universe of all Gods, must be impracticable for Omnipotence
itself."[7]

James Nelson (1710–94), a middle-class apothecary, described the social structure he witnessed in 1753: "Five Classes; *viz.* the Nobility, the Gentry, the genteel Trades (all those particularly which require large Capital),
the common Trades, and the Peasantry."[8] The "peasantry," who are "rustics"
or rural workers, and the working poor of the city were considered "the

---

5. See "British Beehive," which presents and interprets George Cruikshank's *The
British Beehive* etching (London, 1840) through the nine economic and social class levels that were thought to comprise British society. The author concludes: "Cruikshank
appears to have designed the British Beehive as a panegyric to British society, but to
modern eyes it seems a stifling and constricted society, where each person is stuffed
into his or her little compartment. Perhaps unintentionally, Cruikshank managed to
depict a somewhat dystopian society, where the British people are literally worker bees
in a hive" (para. 14).

6. Jenys, *Free Inquiry,* 39.

7. Jeyns, *Free Inquiry,* 40.

8. Nelson, *Essay on the Government of Children,* 273.

lowest Class of People . . . Many are abandoned to vice; many indeed are honest and industrious; but even among those who are themselves good, their children, thro' an early false fondness or the corruption of others, are usually ignorant, untoward, and vicious."[9] Nelson believed the situation of poor children would be improved if "some degree of education [could be provided] the boys; reading, writing, and the first rules in arithmetic at least, which if carefully taught them, will qualify them for many useful employments. The girls should at least read and work at their needle."[10] He affirmed that "in the order of nature, everything has it's own sphere, it's province assigned to it, which cannot be departed from without error, so that in the various degrees of mankind, if a proper regard be not had to situation and abilities, the mistakes committed in educating our children must be very many."[11] For example, "those of an inferior class say . . . 'tis a fine thing to be a scholar!' True, it is so, but surely it is a sad thing to be a learned beggar; and worse to be a learned blockhead; an unlearned cobbler is a prince to either of these."[12]

James Nelson thought the education of children, particularly poor children, should prepare them to be productive citizens *within* the limitations of their class, not in ways that helped them to *transcend* their class. Nelson advocated for universal education, of both boys and girls (albeit differently), but harbored deep prejudices about "rank and station" that created an implicit caste system in Georgian society. Writing in 1790, Rev. John Trusler (1735–1820) viewed the same social hierarchy as a good gift of God that provided order and meaning to all human life:

> Our Creator has ordained that there shall be different ranks and degrees of men . . . It is not that a poor man is less respectable in *his* eyes than a rich man, if he acquits himself well in the state in which it has pleased God to place him; and a poor man never loses his consequence in society, but when he is disorderly and does not fulfil the office assigned him . . . As the servant cannot do without a master; so the master cannot do without a servant . . . They are equal in point of utility, as members of the same society, and subjects of the same state.[13]

It was not always clear to those *men* (and here we mean "men" in a gender-specific way) who gave shape, legitimacy, and even sacred sanction to a

9. Nelson, *On the Government of Children*, 365–66.

10. Nelson, *On the Government of Children*, 366–67.

11. Nelson, *On the Governmetn of Children*, 268.

12. Nelson, *On the Government of Children*, 267.

13. Trusler, *Three Short Letters to the People of England*, II:6. Emphasis original.

hierarchical social order that "the great chain of being" benefited *the few* while it excluded and exploited *the many*. It certainly did not, as James Nelson naïvely suggested, bring them all to "a level" simply because all were "equal in the point of [their] utility." Rev. Trusler's theological endorsement of the God-given social order that made all people "equal in the point of utility" because of their usefulness to society and to God was a theoretical "equality" that doubtlessly was meaningless to those whose lives were devoid of equality and opportunity in the real world.

The Wesley brothers were like an island of equality amidst this ocean of class rank and station. Ward and Heitzenrater rightly describe John Wesley as "the least class-conscious of men."[14] He encouraged the evangelization of the upper class, but preferred not to undertake it himself: "if it were done by the ministry of others."[15] But John Wesley's calling, as he saw it, lay elsewhere: "If I might choose, I should still (as I have done hitherto) preach the gospel to the poor."[16] It was a conviction that shaped the Wesleys' entire approach to ministry. "In the afternoon," John wrote, "I preached near the new square [King's Square]. I find no other way to reach *the outcasts of men*. And this way God has owned and does still own, both by the conviction and conversion of sinners."[17] Charles Wesley's hymnological description of his call to preach sounded the same chord:

> Outcasts of men, to you I call,
> Harlots, and publicans, and thieves!
> He spreads his arms to embrace you all,
> Sinners alone his grace receive;
> No need of him the righteous have,
> He came the lost to seek and save.[18]

Although the Wesley brothers had "the station" and the privileges (education, vocation, and connections) of gentlemen, they behaved in ways that were viewed as an embarrassment to their class. For example, while field-preaching near Gloucester in August 1739, Charles Wesley was accosted by a friend from his college days at Oxford, Mrs. Demaris Kirkham. She stepped suddenly out of the shadows to block Charles's way as he went to address an unwashed multitude: "An old intimate acquaintance . . . stood in my way," he recalled, "and challenged me, 'What! Mr. Wesley, is it you I see? Is it possible that you who can preach at Christ Church, St. Mary's, and etc., should come hither after a mob?' I cut her short with, [this is] 'the work

---

14. J. Wesley, *Journal and Diaries* I:55.

15. J. Wesley, *Journal and Diaries* XXI:IV.233.

16. J. Wesley, *Journal and Diaries* XXI:IV.233.

17. J. Wesley, *Journal and Diaries* IV:427. Emphasis original.

18. C. Wesley and J. Wesley, *Poetical Works* I:92.

which my Master giveth me, must I not do it?"[19] Mrs. Kirkham believed that in his actions Charles betrayed his class and station. She thought Wesley was wrong to go among the poor, that he was a failure and disgrace. But Charles thought he was right with the Divine order of things, as it was established in Jesus' great commission to "go into *all the world* and preach the gospel" (Matt 26:16). "Thousands heard me gladly," Charles reported, as he used his own social privileges to highlight the soteriological privilege of his hearers: "I told them *their privilege* of the Holy Ghost, the Comforter, and exhorted them to come for him to Christ as poor lost sinners. I continued my discourse till night."[20]

The Wesley brothers often disappointed "great" people, who expected the same V.I.P. treatment from the Methodists that they received everywhere else in English society. And so when several "great ladies" requested a private interview with John Wesley after he had given a long and exhausting public presentation, he declined, saying: "You only wanted to *look at* me, [for] I do not expect that the rich or great should want to either speak *with me*, or hear *me*. For I speak plain truth; a thing *you* hear little of and do not desire to hear."[21] While Charles Wesley's personal tastes were less puritanical than Spartan John's, he had no time for the gentrified manners and foppish styles of the fashionable few:

> What is a modern man of fashion?
> A man of taste and dissipation;
> A busy man, without employment;
> A happy man without enjoyment;
> Who squanders all his time and treasures
> In empty joys, and tasteless pleasures;
> Visits, attendance, and attention,
> And courtly arts too low to mention,
> In sleep, and dress, and sport and play,
> He throws his worthless life away;
> Has no opinions of his own,
> But takes from leading beaux the *ton*;
> Born to be flatter'd and to flatter,
> The most important *thing* in nature,
> Wrapp'd up in self-sufficient pride,
> With his own virtues satisfied,
> With a disdainful smile or frown
> He on the riffraff crowd looks down;
> The world polite, his friends and he,

19. C. Wesley, *Manuscript Journal* I:189.
20. C. Wesley, *Manuscript Journal* I:189. Emphasis added.
21. J. Wesley, *Journal and Diaries* II:65. Emphasis original.

All the rest are—no body.

Taught by the great his smiles to sell,
And how to write and how to spell,
The great his oracles he makes,
Copies their vices and mistakes,
Custom pursues, his only rule,
And lives an ape, and dies a fool! . . .[22]

Educational opportunities in Georgian England were profoundly impacted by class, wealth, and privilege. Public education was further complicated by a proliferation of the types of schools available, as well the relatively small number of children who were actually able to attend those schools. The often-repeated generalization that girls and poor children were excluded from formal education is certainly true in the broadest sense. Girls and women lived under restrictive social attitudes and policies that were only beginning to relax in this period (more on this in chapter 7). The poor were excluded formal education because of their lack of funds, proper clothes, and free time. Many poor children worked alongside their parents.

With the gradual emergence of a "middling class," general literacy gradually increased because middle-class people had the time, funds, and opportunity to pursue education for themselves and for their children. The growth of popular literacy throughout the eighteenth century can be measured by the growing popularity of books, lending libraries, and a proliferation of magazines.[23] Lawrence Stone estimated male literacy stood at 56 percent of the population in 1775, while female readers amounted to less than half that number.[24] Most of the Methodist Society Rooms had small libraries and the Methodists entered the world of periodical literature in 1778 through the establishment of John Wesley's *Arminian Magazine*. The Methodists, however literate they were when they started out, gradually became a reading people.

Since there was no governmentally funded primary schools for children, children who learned to read and write did so at home, at a grammar school, or at a charity school. The Wesley children, John and Charles included, received their primary school education at the kitchen table from their talented and practical mother, Susanna Annesley Wesley. From the age of five onwards, Susanna taught the children (*both* boys and girls) to read from the Bible, while their philosophical and somewhat impractical father, Samuel Wesley Sr., taught the boys and a few of the girls Latin, Logic, and

---

22. C. Wesley and J. Wesley, *Poetical Works* VIII:478–80. Emphasis original.

23. Wiles, "Middle-Class Literacy in Eighteenth-Century England," 49–66.

24. Stone, "Literacy and Education in England," 98.

the classics. All the Wesley children learned to read and write well before chores were assigned. The Wesleys' rank and station would have allowed the boys to attend a Grammar School, where they would have learned the rudiments of Latin grammar and other elements of a classical education, but family finances precluded it. Nor was there opportunity for the seven Wesley sisters to attend one of the fashionable Dame schools that taught upper-class girls reading, writing, needlework, and the other skills expected of a proper lady. But at least one of the Wesley girls, Patty, was so well home-schooled that she was able to become a teacher at Mrs. Taylor's Boarding School for Girls in Lincolnshire.[25]

Young men from relatively affluent families were sometimes able to attend private Grammar Schools, which began a boy's classical education. Children of the working poor generally did not attend school at all, but if they did it was often one of the Charity Schools operated by the Church of England which stigmatized them as "the scum of the parish."[26] Since they were "free schools coordinated by the SPCK [Society for the Propagation of Christian Knowledge]," Charity Schools offered a curriculum that served the aims of the Church more than the needs of the students, as Diane Payne, reported: "They did not teach classics nor were they designed as stepping stones to grammar schools or any other type of school."[27] In 1709, 254 Charity Schools enrolled 3,402 pupils, and by 1746 more than 18,000 free schools served 22,258 students,[28] but this was a mere "drop in the bucket" to a population of 6.4 million. Poor children or young people, "the fatherless and friendless," who faced poverty and starvation, as William Morley did in 1729, were often sold into indentured servitude.[29] Morley spent seven years of servitude in colonial Virginia, as did more than 3,000 people a year, for more than a century. Novelist Daniel Defoe drew attention to the sexual exploitation many young women faced during their servitude in his novel *Moll Flanders* (1722).

Alongside of the social stigma attached to those who attended the Charity Schools, "as the scum of the parish,"[30] a debate also raged as to whether working-class children should be educated at all. Bernard Man-deville, author of *The Fable of the Bees*, fueled this debate when he issued the second edition of his popular book with the addition of "An Essay on Charity

25. Clarke, *Memoirs of the Wesley Family*, 517.

26. Payne, "London's Charity School Children," 384.

27. Payne, "London's Charity School Children," 384.

28. Salmon, "Work of the Charity Schools," III:294–95.

29. Grubb, "Fatherless and Friendless," 85–86.

30. Payne, "Charity School Children," 384.

and Charity-Schools" appended to it. Mandeville's arguments *against* educating poor children were fourfold: (1) poor children do not need education to perform the menial jobs they will naturally grow up to do; (2) if they have learning, they will become too proud to work; (3) education allows servants to claim higher wages while at the same time makes them unwilling to do servile work; (4) though it might be reasonable to teach them reading, teaching them to write is completely unjustified.[31] It was not until the Poor Law of 1834 that trade-school education of children was added to the regiment of English workhouses, but *not* reading or writing since it was still debated whether poor children should be literate.[32]

The deplorable state of public education in Georgian England motivated Anglican layman and philanthropist Robert Raikes (1736–1811) to organize "Sunday Schools" for the disadvantaged children of the chimney sweeps who populated his neighborhood. His lay-led, privately funded primary school quickly became a mass movement. Sunday Schools taught literacy and piety through the study of the Bible and the Anglican Catechism. They met *only* on Sundays both before and after Church services, because Sunday was the only day many poor children did not have to work. Sunday Schools were particularly successful in instilling working-class values like literacy, self-discipline, honesty, industry, thrift, improvement, and fair play in their students.[33]

The "public" or "independent schools" of the day were actually elite, privately funded schools which were open to the public only if a student could pay the high fees and acquire the proper recommendations. They were elite prep schools designed to prepare upper-class boys for success at the universities. The Wesley boys attended prestigious boarding schools in London as preteens; John attended Charterhouse School (1714–20) on scholarship, and Charles was at Westminster School (1716–26) where his elder brother, Samuel Wesley Jr., was a tutor. John had few favorable recollections of Charterhouse, but Charles was elected "Captain" of his class and made several lifelong friends, including William Murray, Lord Mansfield, who served as Chief Justice of the King's Bench for more than thirty years. When the aging Charles Wesley relocated his family to Marylebone, London in 1770, he and Murray rekindled their friendship and they were frequently seen walking in the park. The chief justice sometimes visited Charles Wesley's home for impromptu concerts by Charles's musical children, and Mansfield brought

---

31. Neuburg, *Popular Education in Eighteenth-Century England*, 3. Also Mandeville, *Fable of the Bees*.

32. Higgenbotham, "Education in the Workhouse."

33. W. T. Laqueur, *Religion and Respectability*.

his own violin.[34] The "old school boys" network was one of the tacit perks that accompanied rank and privilege. Like most of their prep school class-mates, John and Charles Wesley went up to Oxford, as "Kings Scholars" at Christ Church, where they both earned a master of arts in classics. Oxford and Cambridge, the only English universities at this time, were the purview of the privileged, and down into the mid-nineteenth century as many as 90 percent of the students who attended them were either sons of the landed gentry or of the Church.[35]

Since a person's rank and station in life determined their education, it also impacted their vocation. Women of the gentry and middle class were not expected to have a professional life beyond the domestic roles of lady, wife, and mother. Professions that were of a public nature and required for-mal education were closed to most women. Women occasionally expanded traditional domestic roles into vocations like being governess or teacher at a girls' school. The university, and hence careers in higher education, medi-cine, the law, the clergy, politics, and administrative positions were closed to women and the lower classes. The lack of "preferment," a personal recom-mendation required from a person of high social rank and station, made professional vocations like those in the Church, government, universities, or the military nearly impossible to acquire for those outside the gentry.

The old adage, "it takes money to make money" seemed invariably true in Georgian England because most banks were privately owned, hence the venture capital it takes to start a business was out of reach of all those who did not have personal access to wealth or close friends who had wealth, or who did not own property to mortgage. Commercial banking was still in its infancy and there were fewer than twenty banks in the whole of London of 1750. With the gradual rise of industry, however, as cottage industries moved to factories, a Georgian middle class began to emerge in the trades and in commerce.

The early Methodist responses to the crises created by class prejudice and privilege were many and varied. In the face of the social exclusions many people faced, the Methodists created an inclusive counterculture in the Methodist Society which had only *one* entrance requirement: "The ar-dent desire to flee the wrath to come."[36] Inclusion was at the heart of the gos-pel message they proclaimed, as well as their understanding of Jesus as "The Friend of Sinners," who, even on his cross, "spreads his arms to embrace you

---

34. Tyson, *Assist Me to Proclaim*, 293–94.

35. Gillard, *Education in England*.

36. "The General Rules," in J. Wesley, *Works* VIII:270.

all."[37] Their theological message of acceptance was often mirrored in the life of the Methodist Society where women and men participated on a nearly equal footing and were employed at all levels of the mission. The Society Room was a place where the bow, curtsy, and class-conscious addresses like "ma' Lord, and ma' Lady" were abandoned for the more inclusive language of family: "brother" or "sister." In the intimate fellowship of classes and bands, downtrodden people learned and cultivated a new identity as children of God. Opportunities to testify, serve, and lead gave people of all walks of life dignity and purpose. Not only did they establish free schools like Kingswood for colliers' children, each Methodist Society Room became a locus of education and practical opportunities for uplift.

QUESTIONS FOR FURTHER CONSIDERATION:

1. What can you do to begin faith-based conversations about privilege and exclusion in the twenty-first century? Where do you see this process painfully at work?

2. What should/can you do about it? What can we do about it?

3. What concrete steps can you take to "embrace the outcasts?"

4. What measures of inclusion and uplift can you make available to others?

5. Do you have meaningful work for new people to do, if/when they join your community?

37. C. Wesley and J. Wesley, *Poetical Works* I:92.

CHAPTER 5

"Help Me Make the Poor My Friends"
The Crisis of Economic Disparity

"ENDEMIC POVERTY," WROTE ROY Porter, "was one of the nightmare monsters begat by the Georgian century."[1] The numbers certainly bear this out; in a population of roughly 6 million, over 1 million people fell below the poverty line and were considered "paupers" by Parliament's official standards.[2] This poverty developed even while "enormous energies were expended in grappling with the problem of the poor, against the pressure of soaring rates. In 1700, the cost was between £600,000 and £700,000, and was even then thought to be a disgrace. By 1776, it had shot up to £1.5 million, and then it went through the roof: £2 million in 1786, £4.2 million in 1803.[3] But the demographics communicate very little of the misery that grinding poverty inflicted upon roughly a sixth of the people. England was rapidly becoming "a country of two nations," as described by "the young stranger" in the novel *Sybil*, written by future Prime Minister Benjamin Disraeli:

> Two nations between whom there is no intercourse and no sympathy, who are ignorant of each other's habits, thoughts and feelings, as if they were dwellers in different zones or inhabitants of different planets; who are formed by different breeding, are fed by different food, are ordered by different manners, and are not governed by the same laws . . . the rich and the poor.[4]

1. Porter, *English Society*, 133.
2. Sherwin, "Crime and Punishment in England," 172.
3. Porter, *English Society*, 129.
4. Disraeli, *Sybil* I:149.

Too often the poor were blamed and despised for their poverty, as Samuel Johnson observed in 1738: "All crimes are safe, but *hated* poverty."[5] And so when Charles Wesley prayed, "Help us to make the poor our friends," he and the Methodists were swimming against the tide of public opinion.[6]

John Wesley traveled the length and breadth of England for more than fifty years. He saw more than his fair share of poverty's pain, so he asked: "Why are thousands of people starving, perishing for want, in every part of the nation?[7] The itinerant evangelist looked into the face of poverty more often than most people of his rank and station. There was no denying the misery Wesley had seen "with my own eyes":

> The fact I know; I have seen it with my eyes, in every corner of the land. I have known those who could only afford to eat a little coarse food once every other day. I have known one in London (and one that a few years before had all the conveniences of life) picking up from a dunghill stinking sprats, and carrying them home for herself and her children.
>
> I have known another gathering the bones which the dogs had left in the streets, and making a broth of bones of them, to prolong a wretched life! . . . Such is the case at this day of multitudes of people, in a land flowing, as it were, with milk and honey! Abounding with all the necessities, the conveniences, the superfluities of life![8]

After establishing the fact of epidemic poverty, John Wesley asked the more difficult question: "Why is this? Why have all these nothing to eat?" His answer came close behind: "The plain reason why they have no meat [food] is, because they have no work."[9] Searching for an answer to his own question, Wesley pointed to a series of interlocking economic and political elements that conspired against working people and gradually drove them into poverty. These were people who lived paycheck to paycheck, for whom there was no economic safety net should they be unable to work.

Wesley's list of reasons why working people fell into poverty was a long and diverse one: inflation and shortages drove up the price of products, especially food stuffs, which diminished their marketability. Inflated prices harmed both the farmer and those who bought his produce. John was particularly concerned about the misuse of barley, which was the source

5. Johnson, "London," I:17. Emphasis original.

6. J. Wesley, *Works* XI:55.

7. J. Wesley, *Works* XI:53.

8. J. Wesley, *Works* XI:52–53.

9. J. Wesley, *Works* XI:53.

of cheap bread that was the staple of a working person's diet. Corn, wheat, barley, and other grains were scarce commodities "because such immense quantities of corn [grain] are continually consumed by distilling."[10] The "gin epidemic" hit Georgian England like a tidal wave with horrific health and social effects. So debilitating were the effects of the tons of grain distilled during the the gin craze that Wesley opined that it would be better to to simply dump the grain harvest into the sea instead of turning it into "a deadly poison." He observed: "little less than half the wheat produced in the kingdom is every year concumed, not by so harmless a way as throwing it into the sea, but by converting it into deadly poison that naturally destroys not only the stength, but also the morals, of our countrymen."[11]

With conscientious economic analysis, John Wesley examined the sales tax laws, the use of wheat and barley, as well laws that regulated the production and sale of beef, mutton, poultry, and dairy—each of which seemed to support the interests of the rich and powerful. In the case of beef, the laws created a false scarcity of the product that made prices artificially high. But in the regulation of pork and poultry, poorly considered governmental incentives created such large surpluses that prices fell far below what its producers needed to survive. Wesley also pointed to governmental land tax policies which crushed the freeholder and drove the small farmer into poverty, and the impact of a soaring "national expense"—the cost of empire—which created an unbearable tax burden that fell unevenly upon the working class. "To sum up the whole," he wrote, "thousands of people throughout the land are perishing for want of food. This is owning to various causes; but above all, to distilling, taxes, and luxury. Here is *the evil*, and the undeniable causes of it."[12] Among the solutions John Wesley urged were breaking up monopolies, imposing a luxury tax, and curtailing pork-barrel governmental spending; in short, he advocated the exercise of Christian stewardship on a national level.

Because John Wesley's socioeconomic analysis viewed poverty as a systemic "evil" (or sin), he knew its resolution required a series of system-wide solutions. It is noteworthy that Wesley named this situation an "evil." It was/ is based in self-centeredness and sin; where there is sin, there is culpability involved. But unlike so many of his contemporaries, Wesley did not blame the poor for their own impoverishment. Culpability belonged to those who made laws that favored the interests of the gentry and large land owners at the expense of the freeholder and small farmer, as well as those laws that

10. J. Wesley, *Works* XI:54.

11. J. Wesley, *Works* XI:55.

12. J. Wesley, *Works* XI:57. Emphasis original.

supported the interests of factory owners over the needs and safety of their workers. He viewed exploitive self-centeredness and unjust economic use of privilege as sin—on both individual and national levels. The mandate of Christian stewardship falls equally upon individuals and nations alike; "luxury," fed by runaway consumerism and poor stewardship on the part of a few, often led to the exploitation of many. While John Wesley understood poverty as a moral failing, the failing was not (primarily) located in the deficient character of the working poor. Their impoverishment was largely due to the actions or inactions of others in places of power and positions of authority.

It should be no surprise that poor, hungry, hopeless, and destitute people too often turned to crime. Street crime ranged from "snatch and grab" thefts that made the Georgian era's fashionable wigs a common target, to full-scale food riots and mob violence. In 1720 alone, London was convulsed by public riots so serious and extensive they resulted in criminal prosecution on every second day of the entire year. This was an exponential increase from the previous century, when prosecution for "mob rule" averaged between six or eight times a year.[13] With no official police force, the "peace" was maintained by customary public decorum, sporadic community watch groups, and privately hired watchmen.[14] But these steps did precious little to stem escalating crime and violence.

In the autumn of 1740, for example, Charles Wesley pulled himself out of a sickbed to try to stem the tide of a food riot involving the colliers (miners) in Bristol.

> Above one thousand of them I met . . . The occasion of their rising, they told me, was the dearness of corn. I got [up on] an eminence, and began speaking to them. Many seemed inclined to go back with me to the school [Kingswood, the Methodist School for the miners' children], but the devil stirred up his oldest servants, who violently rushed upon the others, beating, tearing, and driving them away from me.[15]

When a "general assault by the few violent colliers" broke out, the diminutive Charles Wesley strode up to the largest of them:

> I seized on one of the tallest, and earnestly besought him to follow me. That he would, he said, all the world over. About six more I pressed into Christ's service. We met several parties,

13. Shoemaker, "London 'Mob,'" 276.
14. Sherwin, "Crime and Punishment," 177.
15. C. Wesley, *Journal* I:278.

stopped and exhorted them to join us. We gleaned a few of them from every company [of protesters] and grew as we marched along singing to the school."[16]

After three hours of earnest prayer at Kingswood School, they found that "the lion had been chained," and "the leopards were laid down" (Isa 11:6).[17]

The scope of poverty and needs of poor people rapidly outgrew the ability of charities and local churches to alleviate them. The government took notice of these horrific conditions and tried to address them through a series of Poor Relief Acts which sought to aid "the deserving poor." One Act passed in 1720, for example, required all those who sought relief to return to the parish of their ancestral origin. This proved completely impractical for those whose poverty locked them into life in the growing urban ghettos. So eager were some parish authorities to trim people from their poor rolls to avoid having to help them that they forced husbands to sell their wives and children into indentured servanthood before they gave them financial relief.[18]

The Test Act of 1723 required that all those who sought food and shelter reside in workhouses where daily sustenance was exchanged (without pay) for hard labor—which was intended to turn a profit for the operators. Upon visiting a London workhouse in 1797, Sir Frederick Eden reported:

> The workhouse is an inconvenient building, with small windows, low rooms and dark staircases. It is surrounded by a high wall, that gives it the appearance of a prison, and prevents free circulation of air. There are eight or ten beds in each room, they are frequently of flocks and retentive of all scents and very productive of vermin . . . whenever small pox, measles, or malignant fevers make their appearance in the house the mortality is very great.[19]

The workhouses were, essentially, penitentiaries for the needy and sites of genocide for poor children. Roy Porter reported that "of the 2,139 children received into London workhouses in the five years after 1730, only 168 were alive in 1735."[20] By 1776, nearly 2 percent of the entire population of Lon-

---

16. Sherwin, "Crime and Punishment," 177.
17. Sherwin, "Crime and Punishment," 177.
18. Evans, *State of the Poor* II:678.
19. Evans, *State of the Poor* II:678.
20. Porter, *English Society*, 131–32.

don, including men, women, and children, resided across the city's eighty workhouses.[21]

Those people who owned property and therefore had collateral with which to borrow funds ran the considerable risk of indebtedness. Indebtedness was dangerous because a failure to repay one's debts upon request could result in prosecution and imprisonment in one of the many debtor's prisons. The economic fragility of life in eighteenth-century England resulted in the imprisonment of more than 10,000 people each year for indebtedness. Imprisonment, however, did not satisfy the penalty of a person's debts. In fact, their debts continued to grow with interest even while they were imprisoned, and yet their debts had to be paid in full in order to facilitate their release. The incarcerated person was also charged for her/his own upkeep while in debtors' prison.

William Hogarth, *A Harlot's Progress*, Plate 4, 1732, "Moll Beats Hemp in Bridwell Prison," engraving on paper, 29.9 x 37.6 cm, Royal Collection Trust, St. James Palace, London. Used with permission. © Her Majesty Queen Elizabeth II.

Since the imprisoned person was removed from their livelihood, their debts continued to mount while they had no means to earn funds with which to pay them. It was, essentially, a form of state-sponsored extortion. Like a

21. Hitchcock et al., "Workhouses," sec. 6.

kidnapped victim, a debtor's family or friends were forced to pay off their debt if they hoped to see their loved one set free. Since raising one's bail often took a long time, the imprisoned frequently lost their home, farm, business, mine, or whatever stood as collateral on their debt while they were incarcerated. Upon release, many of these people had no means of financial support left. They turned to crime out of utter hopelessness, and their recidivism in crime plunged them into a downward spiral that often led to destruction and death.

With growing poverty, poor relief increased dramatically throughout the Georgian period, but it still fell far short of the need. Drawing from governmental and private sources, poor relief exceeded more than 8 million pounds by the end the century.[22] Porter writes:

> All these responses to poverty fell short because they were treating superficial symptoms, not root causes. What is more, they were handling symptoms locally, when the problems were national. The economy itself, with its exploitive system whereby those who worked hardest got least rewards, was producing a pauper residuum.[23]

When these various efforts failed to break the cycle between poverty and crime, some people, like the evangelical Anglican chaplain and hymnologist Martin Madan (1726–90), advocated for harsher penalties as a deterrent to crime. They argued that severe public punishments, like hanging, would halt the epidemic of street crime. Madan's *Thoughts on Executive Justice With Respect to Our Criminal Laws* (1785) mounted a familiar argument: "The prevention of crimes is the just end of all legal severity; nay, the exerting that severity, by making examples of those just guilty, has no other intention but to deter others, and thus pursue the great end of prevention."[24] Rev. Madan sent a copy of his tract to each of the twelve presiding judges in London, and while one judge wrote back to tell Rev. Madan he was "a cruel and blood thirsty man,"[25] the very same year Madan's tract was published, ninety-seven people were hung in London, often for crimes against property; this was twice the number of hangings than the previous year. William Hogarth's etching, *The Idle 'Prentice Executed at Tyburn*, the second in his series of prints on *Industry and Idleness* (1747), emphasized the importance of "industry," or diligent work, and also illustrated the unfortunate end of

22. Sherwin, "Crime and Punishment," 172.

23. Porter, *English Society*, 132–33.

24. Madan, *Thoughts on Executive Justice*, 11. Arguably, his most famous hymn was "Come Thou Long Expected Jesus."

25. Sherwin, "Crime and Punishment," 182.

those who were idle because they had no work. Peter Forsaith keenly observed that the parson riding with and ministering to the condemned apprentice on his way to the gallows was likely a Methodist since he reads to the felon out of a book labeled: *Wesley.*[26]

William Hogarth, *The Idle 'Prentice Executed at Tyburn: Industry and Idleness,* *Plate 2,* **1747, engraved print, 27 x 40.2 cm, Metropolitan Museum of Art, New York, 32.35 (48).**

It was a clear case of art imitating life, since two months after his "personal Pentecost," Charles Wesley repeatedly visited London's Newgate prison and ministered to poor people incarcerated there. In his journal entry dated July 12, 1738, Charles preached to "the condemned felons," and "visited one of them in his cell, sick of a fever; a poor black that had robbed his master."[27] When Wesley told him of the sufferings of Christ, the love and acceptance of God offered to him, Charles reported that the prisoner showed "all the signs of eager astonishment; tears trickled down his cheeks while he cried, 'What! Was it for me? Did God suffer all these for so poor

---

26. Forsaith, *Image, Identity, and John Wesley,* 74–75.
27. C. Wesley, *Manuscript Journal* I:136.

a creature as me?"[28] For five days, Charles Wesley and his colleagues ministered to these men, and when they rode the cart to their cruel death on the gallows, Wesley rode with them, and in this regard Hogarth's etching reflected real life. Through prayer, spiritual counsel, and hymns of triumphant faith, the prisoners found comfort in the hope of having a future life with God. Many of those who viewed the execution were deeply moved by the men's faith, as Charles reported:

> All expressed their desire of our following them to paradise. I never saw such calm triumph, such incredible indifference to dying. We sang several hymns; particularly, "Behold the Savior of mankind,/Nail'd to the shameful tree"; and the hymn entitled: "Faith in Christ," which concludes: "A guilty, weak, and helpless worm,/Into thy hands I fall:/Be Thou my life, my righteousness,/My Jesus, and my all."[29]

When criminalizing poverty and making horrific examples of those who turned to crime as a path out of their poverty failed to stem the crime wave, a few forward-looking people sought solutions that went to the roots of these problems. One of these solutions resulted in the establishment of the Georgia colony in North America. In 1730, Parliament appointed a blue-ribbon commission to investigate the shockingly high level of crime and criminal recidivism in London and other urban areas. The commission, which was chaired by MP and Christian philanthropist, Gen. George Oglethorpe, reported that much of the criminal activity was caused by deteriorating economic conditions in England's industrializing cities; the growth in recidivism they connected directly to the practices of debtor's prisons. The "Oglethorpe Plan," as it was called, resulted in the establishment of the English Georgia colony as a haven where nonviolent offenders could work off their indebtedness and start a new life. It was no accident that Oglethorpe was a prep school chum of Samuel Wesley Sr., the father of John and Charles, and that both Wesley brothers went to Georgia, in 1736, on a philanthropic ministry.

The early Methodists exercised what modern theologians term a "preferential option for the poor." They did not see the poor as disreputable people to be despised, ignored, or avoided. Instead, the poor were seen as children of God, creatures of sacred worth, whose struggles and pain, rather than signaling their God-forsakenness, often brought them close to God.

28. C. Wesley, *Manuscript Journal* I:136.

29. C. Wesley, *Manuscript Journal* I:139. The first hymn was "On the Crucifixion," composed by Samuel Wesley Sr., and the second was by either John or Charles. Both were originally published in John's *Collection of Psalms and Hymns* (1737).

Many of the early Methodists understood the pains of poverty because, like
the Wesleys themselves, they had experienced it. "O want [lack] of bread,
want of bread!" John wrote. "Who can tell what this means, unless he hath
felt it himself?"[30] While describing the "Heaviness [that comes] Through
Manifold Temptations," John invited his hearers into the life-experience of
the working poor:

> How many are there in this Christian country that toil and labor,
> and sweat, and have it not at last, but a struggle with weariness
> and hunger together? Is it not worse for one after a hard day's
> labor to come back to a poor, cold, dirty, uncomfortable lodg-
> ing, and find there not even the food which is needful to repair
> his wasted strength?[31]

Unlike Martin Madan or the Lords of Parliament, John Wesley was
unwilling to simply blame the poor for their impoverishment. His own life
experience and firsthand observations revealed a fundamental falsehood at
the root of the nation's approach to mass poverty:

> I visited as many more [of the poor] as I could. I found some
> in their cells underground; others in their garrets, half-starved
> both with cold and hunger, added to weakness and pain. But I
> found not one of them unemployed, who was able to crawl the
> room. So wickedly, devilishly false is that common objection,
> "They are poor, only because they are idle."[32]

Contrary to the "common objection," poverty was not often due to
sloth and neglect on the part of the poor, hence John Wesley refused to view
poverty primarily as a character flaw. He knew that the poor were often
industrious and dedicated people who were crushed by debilitating circumstances. His frequent visits among the poor taught John Wesley the same
lesson over and over again: "I visited more of the poor sick. The industry of
many of them surprised me. Several who were ill able to walk, were never-
theless at work; some without any fire, (bitterly cold as it was), and some I
doubt, without any food."[33] Wesley also knew that it was more convenient
for society to blame the poor for their poverty than to take concrete steps
to alleviate it.

Charles Wesley's journal is replete with instances of his visiting the
poor in their distress. Like his elder brother, Charles intended to "make

---

30. J. Wesley, *Sermons* II:228. Emphasis original.
31. J. Wesley, *Sermons* II:227–28.
32. J. Wesley, *Letters II* XX:445.
33. J. Wesley, *Letters II* XX:447.

the poor his friend," and his ministry was strategically planned to work in cooperation *with* them and not simply *for* them. Since the poor are "Jesus' bosom-friends," Charles assumed that any friend of Jesus was a friend of his, and also ours![34] Wesley saw an example of God's preference for the poor in Luke 4:26. It was an example which he and the Methodists intended to emulate:

> The poor I to the rich prefer,
> 　　If with thine eyes I see,
> To bear thy Spirits' character
> 　　The poor are chose by Thee:
> 　The poor in every age and place
> 　　Thou does, O God, approve
> To mark with thy distinguished grace,
> 　　To enrich with faith and love.[35]

Meditating upon Matthew 26:11, "Ye have the poor always with you," Charles Wesley realized that the text was not an expression of the futility of alleviating poverty because the "the poor [are] *always* with you"; rather, it was actually a revelation that the poor represent among us Christ's presence in the world. What we would do for Christ, we should do for the poor. What we would give to Christ, we ought to give to the poor. Charles Wesley wrote:

> Yes, the poor supply thy place
> 　　Still deputed, Lord, by thee,
> Daily exercise our grace,
> 　　Prove our growing charity;
> What to them with right intent
> 　　Truly, faithfully is given,
> We have to our Savior lent,
> 　　Laid up for ourselves in heaven.[36]

Charles's sermons reflected these same insights regarding Christ and the poor:

> You should see and revere your Savior in every poor man you ease, and be as ready to relieve him as you would to relieve Christ Himself. Is Christ hungered? Give Him meat. Is he thirsty? Give Him drink. Is He a stranger? Take Him in. Clothe Him when He is naked, visit Him when He is sick. When He is in prison, come yet unto Him.[37]

---

34. C. Wesley, *Unpublished Poetry* II:404.
35. C. Wesley, *Unpublished Poetry* II:90.
36. C. Wesley, *Unpublished Poetry* II:96.
37. C. Wesley, Sermons, 165.

Searching for short-term solutions to alleviate immediate poverty and hunger, the Wesleys routinely "begged for the poor."[38] They also urged the Methodists to visit the sick and the poor and to step out of their own comfort zone in their advocacy for them:

> You might properly say in your own case, "To beg I am ashamed"; but never be ashamed to beg for the poor; yea, in this case, be an importunate beggar—do not easily take a denial. Use all the address, all the understanding, all the influence you have; at the same time trusting in Him that has the hearts of all men in His hands.[39]

By urging the early Methodists to visit the poor and infirmed, John Wesley was only asking of them to do what he had been doing for nearly fifty years. It was an eighty-two-year-old pastor Wesley who spent his Christmas season visiting the poor:

> At this season we usually distribute coals and bread among the poor of the society [in London]. But I now considered, they wanted [needed] clothes, as well as food. So on this, and the four following days, I walked through the town, and begged two hundred pounds, in order to clothe them that needed it most. But it was hard work, as most of the streets were filled with melting snow, which often lay ankle deep; so that my feet were steeped in snow-water nearly from morning till evening.[40]

Because John Wesley knew poor people firsthand, poverty was not a theoretical discussion for him.

The majority of the eighteenth-century poverty programs, however well intentioned, often had the effect of making the life of the poor worse, not better, and the *de facto* criminalizing of poverty led to greater hopelessness and destitution, and more crime. The Wesleys and the Methodists learned the importance of looking at the larger social context that often connected crime and poverty. While the prevailing culture advocated for a theology that valued things over people, and condoned governmental violence as a deterrent to crime, the Methodists took an opposite route. They valued people more than things, since the Methodists viewed each person as one having sacred worth. They believed that there was no piece of property that was worth the life of a child of God. This theological foundation put the early Methodists on a trajectory to pursue restoration and restitution as

---

38. J. Wesley, *Works* XI:513.
39. J. Wesley, *Sermons* III:390.
40. J. Wesley, *Journal and Diaries* VI:340.

outcomes for criminal behavior instead of the bare retribution of "an eye for an eye." In the infrastructure of the Methodist Societies, they built a sense of community that bred both hopefulness and socioeconomic uplift. And where wrongdoing was perpetrated, they sought to create solutions based in personal renewal and restorative justice, in which lives were salvaged and redirected rather than destroyed.

The constructive responses mounted by the early Methodists were reflected in their "General Rules," where they committed themselves to "doing no harm and doing all the good" they could "to the bodies and souls of men"; and practicing "the means of grace" (*Large Minutes*). In particular, they promised to avoid verbal assault and physical violence. Because of their theology of therapeutic grace and responsible stewardship, they sought to reclaim and renew broken people. They valued people over things, and the lifestyle required by their rules put that commitment into action since they believed that personal holiness and social holiness were inseparably linked. The early Methodists also understood that social crises like equality and the alleviation of poverty and economic justice were everyone's work. Each week, the early Methodists, who were often poor people themselves, collected "a penny for the poor" in their discipleship classes. They worked alongside the poor to develop strategies of uplift and programs of improvement.

QUESTIONS FOR FURTHER CONSIDERATION:

1. How is the Methodists' mantra "Do no harm . . . do all the good you can" reflected in the choices you make and things you advocate for?

2. How does your theology of human identity and Christian stewardship shape the choices you make about the way you live your life and relate to others?

3. Do your thoughts and actions recognize the interconnection between the lack of opportunity and poverty, hopelessness, and crime?

4. Do you advocate for and try to implement programs that opt for approaches based on restorative justice, which has greater benefits for all of society, instead of retributive justice that merely punishes the perpetrator or (too often) the victim of a crime?

5. Do you recognize the severe social crisis caused by mass incarceration (particularly of people of color)? Are you willing to pray, think, and act for the development of better solutions?

CHAPTER 6

"The Methodists Are a Low, Insignificant People"

The Crisis of the Working Poor

JOHN WESLEY'S DESCRIPTION OF the social location of the early Methodists was accurate enough in the broader sense.[1] Typically, the early Methodists came from among the rural or urban laboring poor of the early Industrial Revolution. John Smith's demographic study showed they came from "the upper echelons of the lower classes, and the lower income groups within the middle ranks."[2] An examination of early Methodist class rolls bear this out; for example, one from Newlands (near Newcastle), dated 1745, lists eight domestic workers, seven farmers, two weavers, and a harvester, a laborer, a servant, and one smith.[3] These were hardworking, "blue collar" people who wore cheap cotton clothing which, under the stipulations of the 1720 Woolen Act, had to be dyed navy blue.[4] It seemed important to the Parliamentarians to be able to identify working-class people at a glance as they made laws to support the wool industry.

Many laws like the 1720 Woolen Act intended to extend the paternalist hierarchy of the medieval world into the modern industrializing age. The Georgian era was shaken by the gradual transition from the land-based society rooted in property and patronage controlled by the landed gentry and supported by preindustrial labor, laws, and customs, towards a more

1. J. Wesley, *Works* VI:410.
2. Smith, "Occupational Groups among the Early Methodists," 187.
3. Sugden, "Wesley Class Register," 75–77.
4. Whiteley, *Wesley's England*, 103.

modern, urban, and industrializing society. The old social hierarchy was held together, in part, by subordination and deference on the part of the servants and workers, and patronage and small perks given by the gentry. At the bottom of the social pyramid were the working poor: people "with no property or special skill to shield them from the pressures of the daily struggle for existence."[5] Most of the laboring poor were unskilled day laborers who lived increasingly precarious lives because of the seismic social and economic shifts that were underway. In 1688, unskilled labor made up over half of the population, but they earned less than one-fifth of the national income. By 1803, laborers made up only one-third of the populace due to the greater emergence of trades and a middle class, but they still earned less than one-fifth of the nation's wages.[6] Said simply, statistics gathered by Gregory King (1668) and Joseph Massie (1760) indicate that roughly one-third of all English workers became increasingly impoverished during a time of industrial growth and economic expansion.[7]

The arrival of industry in Georgian England was gradual, as cottage industries grew into factories and mills. The first large-scale factory system is generally said to be Arkwright's cotton mill at Cromford (1771), but records evidence a steady growth of industrial employment throughout the entire century:

> In 1736 two brothers employed 600 looms and 3,000 persons in the Blackburn district; a little before 1750 a Warrington sailcloth manufacturer employed 5,000 persons; in 1758 a small group of Manchester check weavers employed a great many of the weavers of Ashton, Oldham and Royton, and one spoke of employing 500 himself.[8]

It is estimated that as much as one-third of the nation's population made the move from rural to urban life over the course of the century. Records from the Old Bailey, London's court system, show the metropolis grew from roughly a half million in 1670 to over a million by 1801.[9] This pattern of growth was evidenced throughout the country, but it was not uniform; new industrial areas like Liverpool, Birmingham, and Manchester grew rapidly, while traditional agricultural areas in the south and southeast steadily

5. Perkin, *Origins of Modern English Society*, 16.

6. See Perkin, *Origins of Modern English Society*, 16–19, for these demographics and supporting charts.

7. George, *England in Transition*, 14; Mathias, "Social Structure of the Eighteenth Century," 30–50.

8. Perkin, *Origins of Modern English Society*, 87.

9. Emsley et al., "London History," paras. 3 and 4.

declined in population as people relocated to the industrializing mid-lands and mining regions.[10]

The population shift left the people who relocated bereft of the safety net and support of their extended families, ancestral villages, and parish churches. With the rural flight came steadily rising food costs as the availability of farm products gradually declined. At the same time, the abundance of unskilled labor flooding the cities froze wages for the city workers at shockingly low levels. As their meager wages bought fewer groceries and paid less rent in the growing cities, entire families entered the workforce in order to stave off hunger, homelessness, and hopelessness. Hence, John Wesley reported: "Everywhere we find the laboring part of mankind the readiest to receive the gospel."[11] These hardworking people were called the "laboring poor," and it seemed the harder they worked the poorer they became; soon, both parents and all their children worked menial jobs as domestics, or in dangerous jobs in the mills or mines just to hold their lives together. Modern people experiencing "the Wal-Marting of America" have experienced this economic conundrum. It is not surprising that dislocated, hard-pressed people turned to the local Methodist Society to find there a foster family, hope, and help.

A second subtle social transition was underway during the Georgian era as the industrial baron began to supplant the landed aristocrat at the top of the social and economic pyramid. Jonathan Swift saw the change coming when he wrote in 1710, that "*Power*, which, according to the old maxim was used to follow *land*, is now gone over to *money*."[12] As money began to matter more than land, the working poor gradually came to a new and different understanding of themselves; one based less upon the deference associated with their social station and more upon the work they could do or skills they acquired as tradesmen (and women). Writing somewhat satirically in 1724, for example, Daniel Defoe reported the growing insolence and insufferable behavior of workers in *The Great Law of Subordination Consider'd*: "The unsufferable behavior of servants in this Nation is now (it may be hop'd) come to its height; their measure of insolence, I think, may be said to be quite full."[13] As he bewailed the "unsuffereable behavior" of servants and working people who "do not know their place" (so to speak), Defoe's disdain signaled a change was underway:

10. Gilbert, *Religion and Society in Industrial England*, 110–12.

11. J. Wesley, *Journal and Diaries* V:294.

12. Swift, *Examiner*, no. 13, quoted in Cornfield, "Class and Name and Number," 42. Emphasis original.

13. Defoe, *Great Law of Subordination Consider'd*, i.

The poor are . . . idle, proud, and saucy, and when wages are good, they won't work, any more than from hand to mouth; or if they do work, they spend it in riot and luxury; so that it turns to no account to them. While this, then, is the temper of the laboring poor, what are we to expect from . . . they will be mutinous when they want [lack] employment, and idle and saucy when they have it?[14]

In the first letter of the ten that comprised Defoe's "inquiry" into the *The Unsufferable Behaviour of Servants in England,* he spoke through the literary voice of privileged people who enjoyed their rank and station. But as the study unfolded, Defoe's authorial voice shifted to that of a fictional tailor's apprentice, Edmund, who was hauled before the local justice of the peace to answer charges "for breach of covenant or trespass":

Justice: Come in Edmund, I have talk'd with your Master—

Edmund: Not *my Master*, and t'please your Worship, I hope I am my own Master.

Justice: Well, your employer, Mr. E—, the clothier; will the word "Employer" do?

Edmund: Yes, yes and t' please your Worship, I hope *I am my own* Master.[15]

When Defoe's fictional worker rejected the title "master" in favor of "employer," Edmund signaled that a revolution was underway in his own thinking that mirrored the social change underway around him in Georgian England. The long-entrenched medieval conception of the social hierarchy between master and serf that was based in breeding, land, wealth, privilege, and power was being challenged by a new economic hierarchy based on money and skills. The "employer" does not and should not own all of Edmund's time and life, nor own Edmund's soul in the same way his medieval "master" might have. The newer way of looking at their relationship, while still fraught with problems for people like Edmund, challenged the long-held notion that the employer was Edmund's "better." In fact, seen from a very different point of view, one that was championed by the early Methodists, Edmund the tradesman could be, in many ways, a better man than his "master." William Hogarth's painting, "The Servants," captured well the rustic dignity the Methodists saw exemplified in the lives and faces of hardworking people.

14. Defoe, *Great Law of Subordination Consider'd*, 88.
15. Defoe, *Great Law of Subordination Consider'd*, 97. Emphasis original.

William Hogarth, *Heads of Six of Hogarth's Servants,* **c. 1750,**
oil on canvas, 630 x 755 mm, Tate, London. Photograph by Buchman-Hermit.

Raised in a large household on the salary of a rural country parson who was constantly in debt, the Wesley brothers knew the pangs of poverty and understood the weight of economic distress. Doubtlessly, they remembered their father's imprisonment for indebtedness during the summer of 1705, as well as their mother's utter embarrassment at having to write Archbishop Sharpe to beg for funds to secure Samuel Wesley's release.[16] Knowing how easily one fell into poverty, John Wesley felt no particular admiration for people of wealth and status. Too often the general tenor of their lives was an affront to God, he thought, because the wealthy were ungrateful and ineffective stewards of what God had entrusted to them. Wesley believed they merited

> a peculiar curse of God inasmuch in the general tenor of their lives they are not only robbing God continually, embezzling and wasting their Lord's good, and by that very means corrupting their own souls; but also robbing the poor, the hungry, the naked, wronging the widow and the fatherless, and making themselves accountable for all the want, affliction and distress which they may but do not remove![17]

Like the blood of murdered Abel (Gen 4:10), Wesley believed the suffering of the poor, widows, and the fatherless cried out to God against the

16. S. Wesley, *Complete Writings,* 9.
17. J. Wesley, *Sermons* I:628–29.

Georgian gentry: "Yea, doth not the blood of all those who perish for want of what they [the rich] either lay up or lay out needlessly, cry out against them from the earth? O what account will they give to him who is ready to judge the quick and the dead!"[18]

Initially the Wesley brothers preached within and around the edges of the Anglican parish system. But soon the "push-pull" of their calling took them out into the streets, meadows, market squares, village greens, pit heads, and docks, where they met the unchurched people of England. The "pull" was their strong sense of call and vocation "to reform the nation—beginning with the Church," and to "spread Scriptural holiness across the land." The "push" came from the guardians of the old order of patronage and privilege who resented the Wesleys' strong call to repentance and equality nearly as much as they disliked the enthusiasm with which they delivered it.

In the spring of 1739, John Wesley found himself pulled into mass evangelism by George Whitefield. "I could scarce reconcile myself to this *strange way* of preaching in the fields, of which he set me an example," Wesley wrote, "having been all my life (till very recently) so tenacious of every point relating to decency and order that I should have thought the saving of souls *almost a sin* if it had not been done *in a church*."[19] The next day, feeling the call of the gospel and the needs of the people, despite his deep ambivalence, Wesley replaced Whitefield out in the field. John turned to Jesus for encouragement during this departure from "decency and order." He recalled: "I began expounding our Lord's Sermon on the Mount, one pretty remarkable precedent of *field preaching*."[20] Since he had already been "vile" by preaching in a field on the day before, Wesley decided to "be more vile (2 Sam 6:22), and proclaimed in the highways the glad tidings of salvation, speaking from a little eminence in a ground . . . to about three thousand people."[21] Again, following Jesus' pattern, John preached from the text:

> The Spirit of the Lord is upon me, because He hath anointed me to preach the gospel to the poor. He hath sent me to heal the broken-hearted, to preach deliverance to the captives and recovery of sight to the blind, to set at liberty them that are bruised, to proclaim the acceptable year of the Lord. (Luke 4:18–19)[22]

---

18. J. Wesley, *Sermons* I:628–29.

19. J. Wesley, *Journal and Diaries* II:46. Emphasis original.

20. J. Wesley, *Journal and Diaries* II:46. Emphasis original.

21. J. Wesley, *Journal and Diaries* II:46.

22. This passage from Isaiah 61:1 was the text for Jesus' inaugural sermon in the synagogue in Nazareth.

For both preachers, the Lukan text was an inaugural sermon and a mission statement.

Charles Wesley embarked upon the innovation of evangelism *alfresco* from the opposite direction, from *the push* of the Church. When the churchwardens of St. Mary's Church, Islington, where he was the curate, locked arms like a rugby team and blocked his way to the pulpit stairs, Charles spent a prayerful minute in reflection and decided that "the servant of the Lord ought not to strive" (2 Tim 2:21), and resisted the temptation to fight his way through them. After a second similar incident, Charles Wesley walked out of the sanctuary and invited the congregation to join him in the church yard. Roughly half of them did so, and because of its proximity to a major London thoroughfare, the yard was soon teeming with many more people than the church could hold. Charles recalled: "God gave me utterance to make known the mystery of the gospel to four or five hundred listening souls."[23] Two days later, Charles Wesley preached in farmer Franklyn's field, "to about five hundred, on 'Repent, for the Kingdom of heaven is at hand' [Matt 3:2]."[24]

The Methodist innovation of field preaching answered some of the deployment problems that challenged eighteenth-century Anglicanism. If the unchurched populace could or would not come to the church, it seemed obvious that the "Church" should go to them. The Methodist Society did not need an elaborate sacred structure to start up; the use of a parlor, a garret apartment, a storefront, or a barn would do. Hence, their operational overhead was quite low, which allowed them to work among the poor without constantly pressing them for funds. The names of the Methodists' two main urban chapels, the Foundry in London, and the New Room in the Horse Fair, Bristol, both bespoke a history that preceded their use as worship space. The real nucleus of the movement, however, was the network of small groups (bands and classes) that could and did meet almost anywhere. Where Wesleyan mass evangelism claimed a following, Methodist classes were formed, and where several classes were established, a Methodist Society was born.

The needs of the unchurched and the Methodists' stated mission, "to reform the nation—beginning with the Church" made London the starting point but not the terminal location for the movement. After following Whitefield's work in Bristol in the spring of 1739, they met with such huge successes there that Charles Wesley relocated to the thriving port city on

---

23. C. Wesley, *Manuscript Journal* I:172–74, summarizing events between April 28 and May 27, 1739.

24. C. Wesley, *Manuscript Journal* I:174.

the edge of the mining district, and Bristol became the second main hub for the Methodist movement. A preaching house was established in the Horse Fair, and a free school for the children of impoverished miners was established in nearby Kingswood. As they answered "calls" for pastoral service from the north and the mid-lands, the Wesleys traveled there preaching the gospel at strategic locations along the way; in main churches, village centers, cross roads, market towns, and emerging industrial areas. Newcastle upon Tyne, in the northeast, became a third center of Methodist mission because the horrible toll the mining industry took upon its workers necessitated an orphanage there. London, Bristol, and Newcastle were the three corners of the Methodist evangelistic triangle; at least once a year, every year, for nearly fifty years, the Wesley brothers and their lay preachers rode that triangle in a six-hundred-mile circuit that encompassed three-fourths of the entire population of England. As the Methodist movement doubled in size every few years, lay preachers ("assistants") were trained while traveling with the Wesleys and put to work as new branches of the movement were added. Soon, these evangelistic travels were shaped into regular patterns with regular visits. Given John Wesley's penchant for order, it could not have been otherwise, and the Methodist preaching "circuits" were born.

The class meeting was the heart and soul of the Methodist enterprise; in fact, the thousands of people who heard Wesleyan evangelism were not even considered to be "Methodists" until they joined a Society and became members of a small group. The class meeting of ten to twelve people, all of whom lived in the same neighborhood, was a weekly session of spiritual fellowship, pastoral care, and support amidst life's many challenges. The class leader was a mature Christian lay person who shepherded their group through a regiment of prayer, Bible study, hymn singing, and self-examination by urging each one "To speak, each of us in order, freely and plainly the true state of our souls."[25] The class leader was also required "to see each person in his class once a week at least, in order to inquire how their souls prosper; to advise, reprove, comfort, or exhort, as occasion may require; to receive what they are willing to give toward the relief of the poor."[26] The several classes in a town or region met together as a Society at least once a week "in order to pray together, to receive the word of exhortation, and to watch over one another in love, that they may help each other to work out their salvation."[27] The Societies invariably met after worship at their local

25. J. Wesley, *Works* VIII: 270, 272.
26. J. Wesley, *Works* VIII:270.
27. J. Wesley, *Works* VIII:269.

Anglican parish church where the Methodist rules required them to attend and receive the Lord's Supper.

Financing a movement of predominately poor people that was deeply committed to the service of poor people was financially precarious, at best. The Wesleys refused to take up offerings at their evangelistic events, lest it be said that they were in it for the money. The income from selling their many publications—sermons, pamphlets, and hymnbooks—was a mainstay of the movement, as was about half of the stipend gleaned from John's Lincoln College Fellowship. Freewill offerings were collected at Society meetings, and gifts were solicited privately for special needs and special causes. The main collection that occurred through the class meetings was specifically directed to the sustenance of poor people both within and beyond the movement. Since money is often a sensitive matter for people who have little or none, and who feel exploited by the world around them, when funds were solicited by the Methodists it was often done privately. But the sacrificial generosity of the Methodist people was quite remarkable. John recorded one particularly memorable example from Tetney, a village in Lincolnshire:

> [I]n the class-paper (which gives an account of the contribution for the poor) I observed one gave eight pence, often ten pence, a week; another, thirteen, fifteen, or eighteen pence; another sometimes one, sometimes two shillings. I asked Micah Elmoor, the leader . . . "How is this? Are you the richest society in England?" He answered, "I suppose not. But all of us who are single persons have agreed together to give both ourselves and *all we have* to God. And we do it gladly, whereby we are able from time to time to entertain all the strangers that come to Tetney, who often have no food to eat, nor any friend to give them a lodging."[28]

The "Strangers' Friend Society," which was so desperately needed during those times of rural flight and socioeconomic dislocation, soon became a standard philanthropic ministry of each local Methodist Society.[29]

For all his ministerial and administrative business, John Wesley made an amazing number of his own pastoral visits. In his journal, Wesley explained the therapeutic intent of his visitations:

> I visited as many as I could of the sick. How much better it is, when it can be done; to *carry* relief to the poor than *to send* it! And that both for our own sake and theirs. For *theirs*, as it is so much more comfortable to them, and as we may then assist

28. J. Wesley, *Journal and Diaries* III:159. Emphasis original.
29. J. Wesley, *Letters* VIII:261.

them in spiritual as well as temporals. And *for our own* [sake], as it is far more apt so soften our heart and to make us naturally care for each other.[30]

Wesley assumed that the Methodists would follow his logic and example in this matter. Because of their solidarity *with* the poor, the early Methodists were able to engage in attitudes and programs of uplift *for* the poor that were devoid of paternalism. Charles urged the Methodists to be tentmakers like St. Paul, to "use your hands for God" to "work for the weak, sick, and poor":

> Your duty let the Apostle show;
>   Ye ought, ye ought to labor so,
> In Jesus' cause employed,
>   Your calling's works at times pursue,
> And keep the tent-maker in view,
>   And use your hands for God.
>
> Work for the weak, and sick, and poor,
>   Raiment and food for them procure,
> And mindful of his word,
>   Enjoy the blessedness to give,
> Lay out your gettings, to receive
>   The members of your Lord.
>
> Your labor which proceeds from love,
>   Jesus shall graciously approve,
> With full felicity,
>   With brightest crowns your loan repay,
> And tell you in that joyful day
>   "Ye did it unto Me."[31]

Their General Rules committed the Methodists to doing "all they could for the bodies and souls of men . . . according to the ability that God giveth, by giving food to the hungry, by clothing the naked, by visiting or helping them that are sick, or in prison."[32] This was also the aim of John Wesley's famous stewardship dictum: "Gain all you can. Save all you can. Give all you can."[33] His definition of Christian stewardship made the Methodists stewards of the gifts that God had entrusted to them, as well as stewards of the poor: "Be a steward . . . of God and the poor," he declared, "differing from them [the poor] in these two circumstances only—that your wants are

---

30. J. Wesley, *Journal and Diaries* IV:290. Emphasis original.
31. C. Wesley, *Unpublished Poetry* II:403–4.
32. J. Wesley, *Works* VIII:279–80.
33. J. Wesley, *Sermons* I:630.

first supplied, out of the portion of your Lord's goods which remain in your hands; and, that you have the blessedness of giving."[34] Their open hearts and the needs they saw both in their midst and all around them prompted the early Methodist Societies to develop various uplift ministries. In addition to the alms or relief ministered through the stewards, on a local basis, the group provided food, clothing, and lodging for people, as needed. The Societies in London and Bristol, and very likely many other places, had a dispensary which provided rudimentary medical care (based on John Wesley's *Primitive Physick*), patent medicine, and homeopathic healthcare for those who could not afford the attentions of a physician.

The Methodist Rules forbade them from both gambling, and pawning their meager possessions; "Pawn nothing, no, not to save life," both of which were (are) constant banes of the poor.[35] So alongside their provision for short-term sustenance, the Society members pooled their meager funds in order to supply interest-free loans to people who needed a loan to make a fresh start in life. They loaned an older woman enough to buy a cow so she could sustain herself by selling butter and cheese; another young widow was advanced funds enough to buy a small loom so she could weave linen fabric at home while caring for her children; a young man was loaned enough money to buy tools for his apprenticeship.[36] They understood the difference between *giving* someone a fish and *teaching them to fish* (to paraphrase a proverb). With their various ministries, the Methodist movement met the needs of the working poor so well that Maldwin Edwards aptly described them as "the church of the industrial revolution."[37]

The story of John Davis epitomized many others. Davis was a semi-literate, crude, and angry man who enjoyed taunting the Methodist preachers when they came to his town. John Wesley recalled, "For some years John Davis was a mere mule; he would neither lead nor drive."[38] Davis was eventually won to the cause, perhaps through the patient witness of his wife, Anne.[39] Barely able to read when he joined the Methodists, Davis was soon reading his Bible regularly, and eventually he was reading the Bible in its original languages. "To him," Charles Wesley recalled, "godliness was profitable for all things. He had from school no further knowledge than the grammar, but his thirst for a more comprehensive knowledge of all things,

---

34. J. Wesley, *Sermons* I:630.

35. J. Wesley, *Works* VIII:274.

36. North, *Early Methodist Philanthropy*, 118–20.

37. Edwards, *After Wesley*, 86.

38. J. Wesley, *Letters* VII:323.

39. J. Wesley, *Journal* VII:141.

with close study and application, he acquired the knowledge of the Latin, French, Greek, languages."[40] John Davis established the Methodist Bible Society movement so that others could join him in biblical literacy. After sixteen years of class membership, he began to travel with John and Charles Wesley as they mentored Davis into being an effective lay preacher. Charles recalled: "He was strictly just and abounded in works of mercy, so that [even] his enemies who would not freely speak well of him were constrained to say, 'if there was an honest man in the world, John Davis was one.'"[41] Soon thereafter, however, John Davis seemed to fall off the pages of Methodist history. The mystery was solved by an obituary notice reporting the passing of "one John Davis, a native of London, who was employed as a missionary in the West Indies."[42]

As the eighteenth century wore on, the Methodists, aided by the transforming impact of their life together, became economically stable and comfortable. This is borne out by looking at the 1783 class roll from Bristol, in which middle-class people like shopkeepers and tradesmen, and women— like a baker, breecher, brewer, quilter, tailor, and two weavers—outnumbered servants or laborers two to one.[43] That same year, John lamented that in their proliferation of increasingly ornate preaching houses, the Methodists followed the negative example of the early church: "As soon as the heat of persecution was over, and Christians increased in goods, some built Preaching Houses, afterwards called churches. In the following times those that built them were termed *patrons* and appointed whom they pleased to preach in them."[44] Decisions and prerogatives which had previously been solely in the hands of the rank-and-file members of the Methodist Societies began to revert to the whims of their wealthy patrons.

By 1783, the weekly "penny for the poor" was being diverted to ministerial support instead.[45] And by 1787, trustees of the new "City Road Chapel," which was/is quite opulent by Methodist standards, voted (during John Wesley's absence) "that everyone who took a pew should have it for his own."[46] To Wesley, this step toward pew rental amounted to "over-throwing, at one blow, the discipline which I have been establishing for fifty years." He called the same group back together for a second meeting upon his return

---

40. Tyson, "Instrument for Sally," 108.
41. Tyson, "Instrument for Sally," 108.
42. Jackson, *Index to the Memoirs,* 16.
43. J. Wesley, *Journal* VI:447.
44. J. Wesley, *Works* IX:505. Emphasis original.
45. J. Wesley, *Journal* III:300.
46. J. Wesley, *Works* VII:349.

to town the next week, and "after a calm and loving conversation"[47] (one wonders about how "calm" really it was), the earlier ruling was overturned. But the pew rental they left behind in the Church of England began to appear in early Methodism, and soon after John Wesley's death in 1798, the West-Street Chapel in London raised £305 a year through renting pews.[48] Charles Wesley was also concerned that class consciousness had crept into Methodism, and in 1786 he observed:

> Genteelity we now affect,
>   Fond to adorn the outward man,
> Nice in our dress, we court respect
>   And female admiration gain'
> As men of elegance and taste
>   We slight, and overlook the poor,
> But in the rich, with servile haste
>   Contend to make our interest sure.[49]

In 1788, John Wesley's sermon warned of "The Danger of Riches," and he reported what must have seemed like an oxymoron to him: "rich Methodists."[50] The situation was exacerbated by his minimalist view of what it meant to be "rich": "By riches I mean, not thousands of pounds; but any more than will procure the conveniences of life. Thus, I account him as a rich man who has food and raiment for himself and family without running into debt, and something over."[51] Setting the bar for affluence so low allowed Wesley to set the bar of stewardship quite high. But this too was endemic to the Wesleyan "take" on real religion:

> By religion I mean the love of God, and man, filling the heart
> and governing the life. The sure effect of this is the uniform
> practice of justice, mercy, and truth. This is the very essence of
> it, the height and depth of religion, detached from this or that
> opinion, and from all particular modes of worship.[52]

It was with a hint of wonder and some satisfaction near the end of his ministry that John Wesley recalled, "Near fifty years ago . . . Two or three *poor people* met together in order to help each other to be real Christians. They increased to hundreds, to thousands, to myriads, still pursuing their one

47. J. Wesley, *Works* VII:349.
48. Telford, *Two West-End Chapels*, 77–78.
49. C. Wesley, *Unpublished Poetry* II:44.
50. J. Wesley, *Works* III:527–28.
51. J. Wesley, *Sermons* II:560.
52. J. Wesley, *Sermons* III:448.

point, real religion, the love of God and man ruling all their tempers, and words and actions."[53]

QUESTIONS FOR FURTHER CONSIDERATION:

1. Do you think of Christian stewardship in the broad terms suggested by your membership vows in which you promised to "do all the good you can for the bodies and souls of men?"

2. Do you endeavor to make friends of the poor, and/or others who are different from yourself as a part of your Christian vocation? How and why might you do that?

3. Do you pause to reflect upon how issues like class, privilege, race, or gender affect your life, your faith, and your outlook on others and your actions?

4. Are you making time and opportunity to get to know and work *with* others who differ from you? To pray and dream about creating new missional works?

5. Do you see concerns like finances, popularity, and acceptance shape the direction of your own Christian life and that of your faith community? How?

53. J. Wesley, *Sermons* III:453. Emphasis original.

CHAPTER 7

"Like a Mother in Israel"

The Crisis of Women's Equality and Exclusion

THE WOMEN OF GEORGIAN England found themselves, to greater or lesser degrees, in the firm grip of a patriarchal social structure that reached back almost two millennia to the ancient Greeks. Social norms based on patriarchy fit well with the "one great chain of being" philosophy that put women under the authority and protection of men by relegating them almost entirely to the domestic sphere of life in the kitchen and the bedroom. The arrival of the Age of Reason, latitudinarian Anglican theology, nascent industrialism, and the gradual emergence of an English middle class during the eighteenth century each in their own way weakened the grip of the old social order. But Georgian women of all classes still lived within the framework of "the domestic ideal," although they often lived very differently. The span of options for their lives was represented by two dichotomous symbols: "the ideal lady" and "the drudge." Either way, as Daniel Defoe reminded his readers, "the good treatment of wives in England is not such as may be boasted of at present."[1]

The ideal lady's life was defined by "the cult of true womanhood." While often associated with Victorian England, this ideal was well in place in the Georgian era. The life of a "proper" woman was, as described by Barbara Welter, shaped by four cardinal virtues: "The attributes of True Womanhood, by which a woman judged herself and was judged by her husband, her neighbors and society could be divided into four cardinal virtues: piety, purity, submissiveness and domesticity."[2] "Religion or piety was the core of

---

1. Defoe, *Great Law of Subordination*, 3.
2. Welter, "Cult of True Womanhood," 152.

woman's virtue . . . Religion belonged to woman by Divine right, a gift of God and nature."[3] Hence, eighteenth-century women were often viewed as the spiritual force of their homes, and as spiritual guides to their children. Among the gentry, in particular, this meant that men could and often did abdicate their spiritual role and live by a double standard that gave them moral and sexual license their wives would never have. Susanna Annesley Wesley (1669–1742), the illustrious mother of John and Charles, was a prime example of a person who took up the role of spiritual guide and mentor to her children. In fact, she left a long list of written instructions describing the precise methods she employed in the ministry of raising her ten children because John Wesley wanted to learn from her as he built the curriculum for this Kingswood School.[4]

Since women were barred from formal education and from active involvement in the public sphere, most professional careers were closed to them. Linking the two important spheres forbidden to women, Lady Mary Montagu (1689–1762) observed that most men of the age regarded education for women "as great a profanation as the clergy would do if the laity should presume to exercise the functions of the priesthood."[5] But the Georgian world witnessed an increase in educational opportunities for women, and an army of Methodist laity (men and a few women) exercised many of "the functions of the priesthood."

The "cult of true womanhood" strongly adhered to women of the gentry and to those women who aspired to the sort of respect and deference that went with nobility. The ideal lady was a woman on a pedestal to be admired by all, a paragon of decorum and virtue, and an inspiration in her wit and etiquette. She was often accoutered with all the material trappings of success. But a bird in a gilded cage is still a bird in a cage, so John Wesley urged the newly minted Methodist, Miss Marsh, "Put off the gentlewoman. Go to the uneducated poor. Creep in among them in spite of dirt and a hundred disgusting circumstances."[6] Wesley told Miss Marsh, in effect, to come down off her pedestal if she intended to be of any good to God, to others, or to herself.

Often an "ideal woman" needed to remain in her "proper place" or forfeit what influence and small opportunities she might have for self-determination. Selina Hastings, the Countess of Huntingdon (1707–91) was a "peer of the realm," who upon becoming a Methodist in the early 1740s

3. Welter, "Cult of True Womanhood," 152.

4. S. Wesley, *Complete Writings*, 367–77.

5. Montagu, *Letters*, 416.

6. J. Wesley, *Letters* VI:207.

parlayed her aristocratic privileges and wealth into religious leadership. She gradually became the matriarch over a "Connexion" of sixty-seven chapels arranged into twenty-three circuits.[7] But she worked behind the scenes in the sphere of administrative leadership. The Countess rarely went public with her leadership and she often camouflaged it with the more acceptable language of weakness and deference.[8] To her most illustrious chaplain, George Whitefield, Lady Huntingdon was "acting the part of a mother in Israel more and more. For a day or two, she has had five clergymen under her roof, which makes her Ladyship look like a good Archbishop, with his chaplains around him."[9] Despite her many accomplishments, however, Lady Huntingdon was handicapped by the handwriting she aptly described as a "miserable scrawl." It was her inheritance from the absence of an early education.[10]

Since land was wealth and power, marriages among the gentry were often arranged like land contracts. The aristocratic women were expected to embrace a marriage that would guarantee their social standing and financial security—along with that of their families. And so John Wesley's flirtatious "spiritual friendship" with vivacious Mary Granville during his days at Oxford came to an end when his lovely, seventeen-year-old "Varanese" wound up in an arranged marriage with sixty-year-old Alexander Pendarves in 1717. Widowed seven years later, Mary "moved with serene dignity and graceful propriety among the most brilliant and refined English society, a true genius in the art of living."[11] John Wesley corresponded with Mary even after her marriage, and with enough warmth to make both Mary and his family uncomfortable with his familiarity.[12] Mary's love would not be the last opportunity to elude him.

The well-accepted nurturing and spiritual roles of women's domestic life, alongside the changing religious landscape, allowed a few women to take cautious and socially subversive steps towards education, literary ventures, and teaching positions at private schools for children, as well as informal and unpaid service in the church. By mid-century, small groups of intellectual and literary women, like Mary Montagu, "the queen of the Bluestockings," met with like-minded men for searching conversation about literature, politics, philosophy, and ythe important topics of the day. They

7. Tyson, "Lady Huntingdon's Reformation," 580–93.

8. Tyson, "'Poor Vile Sinner,'" 107–19.

9. Whitefield, *Works* II:380–81.

10. Tyson, "Lady Huntingdon's Reformation," 581.

11. Myers, "Mrs. Delany," 12. The story of Mary Granville, née Pendarves, née Delany is an interesting one.

12. Rack, *Reasonable Enthusiast*, 78–79.

were called "bluestockings" because these were socially casual events, where the quality of the conversation mattered more than formal attire. Mary Granville (aka Mrs. Delany) and Martha Wesley Hall, the literary elder sister of John and Charles who was always inexplicably called "Patty," participated in a similar group that revolved around the eminent Dr. Samuel Johnson.[13] Selina Hastings turned her bluestocking events into "drawing room evangelism" by adding a few Methodists like George Whitefield, Charles Wesley, William Romaine, or John Fletcher to the guest list, along with her aristocratic friends.[14] The gradual Georgian appreciation of women's rights and abilities seemed to reach its apex at the end of the century with the publication of *A Vindication of the Rights of Women* in 1792 by Mary Wollstonecraft (1759–97). Methodism played a significant role in that development.

The cult of true womanhood also had the effect of turning lower-class women into menial "drudges" who were chained to the house or locked into wage-slavery in a mill. Their poverty, incessant work, lack of education, and lack of opportunities defined their lives. Married before the age of twenty, lower-class women could expect to have six children, at least two of whom would die in infancy. They would be expected to juggle raising children, keeping a house on very meager funds, and trying to bring in extra income as long as they could manage it. The life of a single woman was even more challenging; with little or no education and few marketable skills, she often lived payday to payday doing menial and often dangerous work. If she was a part of the rural exodus, her life was even more precarious because she was living far from home in the city, without a safety net. Writing in 1725, the ever-observant Defoe reported that "this is why our streets are swarming with strumpets . . . [who] make neither good *whores* nor good *servants*,"[15] and, as Lawrence Stone pointed out, "those were the only two major occupations open to an uneducated girl from a poor family. Because of the irregularity of employment, the two often tended to get mixed up."[16] This sad situation seemed to validate "Place's Law," that "poverty and chastity are incompatible" in eighteenth-century England.[17] A survey conducted by Justice John Fielding in 1768 found that the majority of London's working girls, aged 14–25, were sexually abused while trapped in domestic employment, and occasionally turned to prostitution to supplement their income.[18] The trauma produced by this tragedy was incalculable.

13. Maser, *Seven Sisters in Search of Love*, 79–101.

14. Tyson, "Lady Huntingdon's Reformation," 587–88.

15. Defoe, *Everybody's Business Is Nobody's Business*, 5. Emphasis original.

16. Stone, *Family, Sex, and Marriage*, 617.

17. Stone, *Family, Sex, and Marriage*, 616–18.

18. Stone, *Family, Sex, and Marriage*, 616–18.

William Hogarth, *A Harlot's Progress, Plate 1*, **1732, print, 31.3 x 38.4 cm, Royal Collection Trust, St. James Palace, London. Used with permission. © Her Majesty Queen Elizabeth II.**

William Hogarth, *A Harlot's Progress, Plate 6*, **1732, print, 31 x 38.3 cm, Royal Collection Trust, St. James Palace, London. Used with permission. © Her Majesty Queen Elizabeth II.**

William Hogarth explored the making of a prostitute in a series of six paintings and etchings entitled "A Harlot's Progress" (1732). Hogarth's heroine, "Moll Hackabout," was depicted as a victim of a series of unfortunate events rather than a willful perpetrator of wrongdoing. In the first painting, in which Moll arrived in the city on the back of a market wagon, she looks innocent, hopeful, and naïve. Moll's dream for a better life in the city soon took a cruel detour through life in a brothel because she mistakenly put her trust in the madam who met her in the market square. Her detour ended in Bridwell, a debtor's prison (plate 4), where, diseased by syphilis (plate 5), she died. Her funeral (depicted in plate 6), was officiated by a lewd parson who was busily groping one of the attendees; the only other mourners at Moll's wake were a former "John," three of her co-workers, and her young, orphaned son.

John Wesley's vagabond evangelistic life taught him more about the plight of prostitutes than most proper clergymen knew or cared to know. His *A Word to an Unhappy Woman* (1745) crystalized Wesley's message to the street-walkers he encountered on a regular basis. His euphemism for describing them, "Unhappy Woman," is revealing since, instead of calling them "whores," "harlots," "prostitutes," or worse, Wesley saw these women as victims of cruel circumstances which forced them to make "unhappy" choices. His message to these women was not full of blame and condemnation; rather, he urged their restoration through finding a new identity for themselves as children of God, and with this new beginning they could make as ones forgiven and renewed by God's love. Wesley acknowledged the life in which they found themselves was a living hell, and urged them to make different life choices because the road they were traveling led only to the utter destruction of body and soul: "This instant, now, escape from your life; stay not; look not behind you. Whatever you do, sin no more; starve, die, rather than sin. Be more careful of your soul than your body. Take care of that too; but of your soul first."[19] To the woman's hypothetical reply, "I have no friend, and none who is able to help me," John Wesley reminded her that afflicted and rejected people always have a friend in the rejected and afflicted One, Jesus Christ.[20] Given the fact that this gospel word came from an eminent Methodist evangelist, it was implicit that Wesley's intention was that this "unhappy woman" would not only find a friend in Jesus, but she would also find many friends in the restorative fellowship of "the people called Methodists."

19. J. Wesley, *Works* XI:172–73.
20. J. Wesley, *Works* XI:173.

Growing up in a home with their remarkable mother and seven talented sisters gave John and Charles Wesley a countercultural estimate of the abilities and equality of women. It is easy to imagine that John and Charles Wesley developed their unconventional views having learned to read their Bible at the knee of Susanna Annesley Wesley, watching her lead an "evening prayers" meeting in their home for more than 200 people while their pastor-father was away, or seeing her publish *Some Remarks on a Letter from the Rev. Mr. Whitefield to the Rev. Mr. Wesley in a Letter from a Gentlewoman to Her Friend* (1741) when she felt that the eminent evangelist had slandered her son(s). The Wesley brothers were also comfortable with women's friendship in ways many of their male contemporaries often were not. Their communications with women were respectful, thoughtful, not condescending; friendly without being colored by conquest. Their Moravian friend James Hutton observed the way his own sisters responded to the Wesley brothers and described them both as "snares to women," and urged them both to marry. Charles did marry, and happily. John was less adept at relationships; he did not marry several times, before he finally did marry, but unhappily.

Class rolls demonstrate that women populated Methodist Societies, classes, and ministries two or three times more often than men. Perhaps this was to be anticipated since piety was one of the virtues the Georgian world assigned to its women. But the equality (both spiritual and practical) and the opportunities women experienced among the Methodists were factors in the movement's attraction for them. The Methodist Society was an alternative culture and a spiritually liberating social sphere where women had greater equality, affirmation, and opportunities than were accorded in the larger, outside world.

The terminology the early Methodists used among themselves reflected their theology of equality and inclusion; rather than employing the language of deference, reinforcing the attitudes of the hierarchical culture, the early Methodists turned to the familial language of "sister" and "brother" to encourage a rethinking of all relationships. Their affirmation of the "spiritual equality" of women and men, for "there is neither Jew nor Greek, there is neither bond nor free, there is *neither male nor fe*male: for ye are all one in Christ Jesus" (Gal 3:22; emphasis added), also led to practical equality. It was evidenced by the specific roles women played as leaders of small groups, witnesses called forth to speak or testify to their Christian experience, officers in the Society, and directors of significant Methodist ministries (like the Orphan House in New Castle), and eventually as lay preachers. And as we saw in John Wesley's words to Miss Marsh (above), these opportunities also led to the realization that in order to do the Christian service (the work of a deacon), she would need to forfeit her identity as a "gentlewoman" and take on a new identity as "servant." Many of Charles Wesley's hymns celebrate and eulogize the servant lives of early Methodist women, like Mrs. Mary Naylor, who was like "a mother to the poor" and gave poor people her "ministerial aid":

> The golden rule she has pursued,
> And did to others as she would
>   Others should do to her;
> Justice composed her upright soul,
> Justice did all her thoughts control,
>   And formed her character.
>
> Affliction, poverty, disease,
> Drew out her soul in soft distress,
>   The wretched to relieve;
> In all the works of love employed,
> Her sympathizing soul enjoyed
>   The blessedness to give.
>
> Her Savior in his members seen,
> A stranger she received him in,
>   An hungry Jesus fed,
> Tended her sick, imprisoned Lord,
> And shew in all his wants to afford
>   Her ministerial aid.
> A nursing-mother to the poor,
> For them she husbanded her store,
>   Her life, her all, bestowed;
> For them she labored day and night,
> In doing good her whole delight,
>   In copying after God.[21]

These ministering women were said to be "like a mother in Israel." The term described the way these women fulfilled and greatly exceeded the "motherly" roles prescribed for them by eighteenth-century society. But they also dramatically expanded those private domestic roles into public ministries. The phrase "like a mother in Israel" was borrowed from "the Song of Deborah" in Judges 5:9, where Deborah, the female judge and leader of the nation, celebrated the effect she saw as God's power worked in and through her life. The phrase also suggests one might expect something more than the normal domestic ideal from a Methodist "mother in Israel." Indeed, this was precisely the case.

21. C. Wesley, *Journal* II:238–39.

Grace Murray (1718–1803) was, as Paul Chilchote described her, "a prototype for female leadership in early Methodism."[22] Grace came to faith in the early years of the revival, and was listed as one of the female band leaders at London Society that met at the Foundry. She soon was spiritual guide and mentor to more than 100 people, who met with her in several separate groups. When John Wesley established the Orphan House and northern headquarters in New Castle (1742), Grace went north to be mistress in charge of that work. From there, her early biographer reported, Grace "traveled by Mr. Wesley's direction, through several of the northern counties, to meet and regulate the female societies; afterwards she went over to Ireland for the same purpose."[23] Her vibrant ministry was based in domestic virtues like hospitality and spiritual nurture, aspects of being an "a true woman" that were extended into the public sphere. She was "a mother in Israel," who became John Wesley's "fellow laborer in the gospel."[24]

Grace Murry also traveled with John Wesley as a pastoral assistant. She recalled: "Mr. W. took me with him into several places in the Country; and I found a continual increase of Hope. And I never wanted [lacked] Power from God to pray with and labor among the People."[25] After Grace nursed Wesley back to health from a near-fatal illness, she traveled with him again for six months, during which time he developed a romantic attachment towards her based in part upon Ms. Murray's effectiveness as "a fellow laborer in the Gospel." "As to the fruits of her labors," John recalled "I never yet heard or read of any woman so owned of God: So many have been convinced of sin by her private conversation; and so many have received remission of sins in her bands or classes or under her prayers."[26] J. A. Leger described John's affection for Grace Murray as *John Wesley's Last Love*, whether that is true or not, John's subsequent marriage to Mrs. Mary Vazeille in 1751 was a disaster.

Scores of Methodist women took on leadership roles by following a path similar to that trod by Grace Murray. Sarah Perrin, for example, became John Wesley's administrative assistant in Bristol, where she managed the house and kept the books;[27] and like Grace Murray, her ministry sometimes expanded into exhorting or testifying to her faith.[28] In Weardale, Jane

---

22. Chilcote, *Her Own Story*, 71.
23. Chilcote, *Her Own Story*, 71.
24. Chilcote, *Her Own Story*, 71.
25. Leger, *John Wesley's Last Love*, 53.
26. Leger, *John Wesley's Last Love*, 73.
27. J. Wesley, *Journal and Diaries* II:462.
28. Lloyd, "Sarah Perrin," 79–88.

Salkeld, "a young woman that is a pattern to all that believe," developed an impactful children's ministry that planted and nurtured faith in forty-three young souls.[29] When he visited Weardale ten years later, John Wesley reported "that mother in Israel, Jane Nattrass (before Salkeld, the great instrument of that amazing work among the children)" had died, but her work lived on, since "God is with *them* still."[30]

The story of women in American Methodism began in the prerevolution British colonies with European immigrants like Barbara von Ruckle Hescht (1734–1804), who came to North America and brought their Methodism with them. Barbara made a profession of faith under the impact of Wesleyan evangelism and subsequently emigrated to America (in 1760) with her husband Paul Hescht (pronounced Heck), her cousin Philip Embury, and several others. Soon after their arrival in New York City, Barbara was shocked and distressed by the godless effect of the city upon her people; she even witnessed Methodists playing cards! With characteristic directness, she turned to Philip Embury, who had been a Methodist lay preacher in Ireland, to begin a class meeting in his rented house. "Philip," she is reputed to have shouted, "you must preach to us or we shall all go to hell together, and God will require our blood at your hands!"[31] Their first class meeting was comprised of five people; the Heschts, a man-servant, and an African-American domestic named Betty.[32] The class soon grew into a Methodist Society, and by 1768, they had moved to a new chapel on John's Street, the first Methodist church in New York City.[33]

Women were prominent in establishing a Methodist ministry in Philadelphia where Mary Thorn was converted to Methodism from her Baptist leanings after hearing the traveling preacher Joseph Pilmore preach at a Society meeting. She soon became a class leader there, as well as a passionate participant in revivals. Mary Wilmer and Hannah Baker also joined Mary as class leaders. When Methodism came to Annapolis, Maryland in the 1780s, the founding members of the first Society there were all women.[34] And these pioneering women leaders nurtured their families in the faith: "One by one," wrote Dee Andrews, "the daughters and granddaughters of the itinerants' first female advocates joined the movement."[35] As the

29. J. Wesley, *Journal and Diaries* VI:334.
30. J. Wesley, *Journal and Diaries* II:316. Emphasis original.
31. Withrow, *Barbara Heck*, 30.
32. French, "Ruckle, Barbara (Heck)."
33. Andrews, *Methodists in Revolutionary America*, 160.
34. Andrews, *Methodists in Revolutionary America*, 100–101.
35. Andrews, *Methodists in Revolutionary America*, 104.

Methodist itinerant preachers made their arduous rounds, their ministries were supported and sustained by the hospitality of many "mothers in Israel" like Mary Thorn, Mary Wilmer, and Hannah Baker. Mary Thorn, for example, was such a great encouragement to Francis Asbury (1745–1816) and his ministry that they corresponded after even her family returned to England. In one such letter, Bishop Asbury reminisced: "Surely you sometimes think how often we have sat and talked together at your own house and the houses of others, about the precious things of God."[36]

J. C. Buttre, *Catherine Livingston Garrettson,* c. 1790, ink engraving, 30.73 x 41.42 cm, General Commission on Archives and History of The United Methodist Church, Madison, New Jersey.

Catherine Livingston Garrettson (1752–1849) epitomized the American version of "a mother in Israel" through her "ministry of public domesticity."[37] Born into one of the wealthiest families in colonial America, Catherine Livingston was converted to Methodism through reading books by John Wesley—at the suggestion of one of her household servants. She married Freeborn Garrettson, one of the most prominent Methodist preachers of the era, in 1793, and turned their home, "Traveler's Rest," on the Hudson River, into a haven of hospitality and spiritual renewal for traveling preachers and visitors of all sorts.[38] Her fully orbed ministry was, as Diane

36. Asbury, *Journal and Letters* III:156.
37. Lobody, "Wren Just Bursting Its Shell," 28.
38. Moore, "Catherine 'Kitty' Livingston Garrettson," para. 1.

Lobody described it, both "entirely acceptable as a feminine enterprise and yet as vibrantly pastoral as any man's ministry."[39]

During the same period, Mary Morgan Mason (1791–1868) extended women's traditional nurturing and teaching roles by pioneering the Sunday School movement in New York City (1815) among the Methodists. For more than thirty years, "She brought up children. She lodged strangers. She relieved the afflicted. She diligently followed every good work."[40] Mason was instrumental in the founding the New York Female Missionary Society in 1819, and under her leadership the Society moved beyond it's auxiliary role (to the male-dominated Mission Society) and extended its own works to the Wyandott Nation in Ohio during the 1820s, and then to Liberia, West Africa in the 1830s.[41]

A second Mary in ministry, Mary Clarke Nind (1825–1905), developed a western branch of the Methodist Female Mission Society. She and her husband emigrated from England and relocated to the American Midwest where she was dramatically affected by the great revivals there. As her own sense of call and gifts for ministry grew, a friend suggested: "Mrs. Nind, we shall all miss you if you decide to leave the Congregational Church; but if I were you I would go into the Methodist Church. You will be more happy and more useful there, for there is more liberty for women to exercise their gifts."[42]

Initially, Mary Nind affiliated with the Free Methodist Church, but upon relocating to Winona, Minnesota she joined the Methodist Episcopal Church and became one of the founding member of the Women's Foreign Missions Society in 1870. In 1888, the Minnesota Annual Conference elected Mary Clarke Nind to be a delegate to the Methodist Episcopal General Conference. But when she and Frances E. Willard, Amanda C. Rippley, Angie F. Newman, and Elizabeth D. Van Kink presented their credentials as duly elected representatives to that legislative session, they were denied admission to the meeting because the MEC *Discipline*'s stipulated that "only duly elected lay*men*" could serve as representatives, which literally meant "men" and therefore excluded "women." Relegated to the balcony, the five females fought for women's full inclusion in the church's legislative process. Of the five excluded women, only Nind lived to see the day when "lay women" were granted full inclusion in the Methodist General Conference in 1904. Although none of these early "mothers in Israel" women preached in

39. Lobody, "Wren Just Bursting Its Shell," 29.
40. Warrick, "'She Diligently Followed Every Good Work,'" 214.
41. Warrick, "'She Diligently Followed Every Good Work,'" 219–23.
42. Nind, *Mary Clark Nind and Her Work*, 21.

the formal sense, soon others would. As we shall see in another section, the emergence of female preachers sorely tested the extent of women's equality within Methodism.

QUESTIONS FOR FURTHER CONSIDERATION:

1. Is your community of faith open to the gifts and needs of women and others whom our dominant culture excludes or pushes to the margins?

2. Does your theology of the "spiritual equality" of women and men take expression in the composition of leadership teams, the delegation of responsibilities, and offices?

3. Does the language you use to describe or to address members of the community (including women) reflect your desire to include and empower everyone?

4. What concrete steps can you take to help further the causes like the inclusion and equality of women (and all people)?

5. In what ways can you work within the existing boundaries placed upon our lives and, like "mothers in Israel," extend those into exciting new opportunities?

CHAPTER 8

"Give Liberty to Whom Liberty Is Due"

The Crisis Caused by Racial Prejudice

MODERN HISTORIAN GRETCHEN HOLBROOK Gerzina described a day in which she found herself in a London bookstore looking for a book on the early history of black people in Britain. When she could not locate it, she turned to the saleswoman for assistance. "Madam," she was told, "there *were* *no* black people in England before 1945."[1] Although people of African descent had lived in Britain since the Roman period, the clerk's answer was not as naïve as it might seem. The "paucity of historical artifacts" and various other issues have made the discovery of black history in Britain challenging.[2] Hence, hard numbers about black presence in Georgian England are difficult to find; estimates generally settle on the 20,000 black residents of London mentioned in *The Gentleman's Magazine* of 1776.[3] This amounted to about 3 percent of the city's populace. Bristol and Liverpool were also leading centers of England's slave trade and had a sizeable population of black Britons, most of whom were slaves who worked as domestic servants.[4]

In the Georgian era, the buying and selling of people of African descent was so common that advertisements regularly appeared in local newspapers: "A negro man aged about 20 years, well limb'd, fit to serve a gentleman or be instructed in a trade."[5] The advertisement also offers a hint about the role of

1. Gerzina, *Black London*, 3. Emphasis oiginal.
2. Blain, "Enslaved People in Eighteenth-Century Britain," paras. 4–5.
3. Edwards, "History of Black People in Britain," para. 1.
4. Jones and Youseph, *Black Population of Bristol*.
5. Jones and Youseph, *Black Population of Bristol*, 5.

black people in Georgian society; they were often domestic servants, not the field hands of the American South. In England, farm labor was done by white indentured people who could be obtained more cheaply, while well-attired black servants were often fashion statements for the rich gentry.[6] Whatever their circumstances, however, "slaves brought to London as servants were in a particularly ambiguous position, as the law neither clearly recognized the legality of slavery, nor granted them freedom from it. As a result many black domestic servants were left to the limited mercies of their employers."[7] Runaway slaves were sought, with some frequency, by slave catchers through advertisements placed in the London newspapers.[8]

Thomas Gainsbourgh, *Ignatius Sancho, An African Man of Letters,* **1768, oil on canvas, 73.7 x 62.2 cm, National Gallery of Canada, Ottawa, Ontario. From Wikimedia.**

A few exceptional black Britons were *very* visible in eighteenth-century England. Ignatius Sancho (1729–80), a former slave who became "An African Man of Letters,"[9] had the distinction of being painted by the famous artist Thomas Gainsbourgh, and his portrait hangs in Canada's National Gallery. Julius Soubise (1754–98) was a Caribbean-born slave, given a lavish life by Catherine Douglas, Duchess of Queensbury. He was frequently caricatured as a very stylish black man fencing. Francis Barber (1735–1801)

6. Emsley et al., "Black Communities," para. 6.
7. Emsley et al., "Black Communities," para. 6.
8. Corlet, "Between Colony and Metropole," 42–44.
9. Sancho, *Letters,* 1.

achieved notoriety as a slave who became the assistant and then heir of the literary Dr. Samuel Johnson. And a former slave from Ghana, Ottobah Cugoano (1757–1803), published one of the first abolitionist books written by a black man in 1787.[10]

Phyllis Wheatley, **1773, frontispiece, London.**

Rev. John Marrant, **1791, thumbnail sketch.**

10. Cugoano, *Thoughts and Sentiments on the Evil and Wicked Traffic of the Slavery*

Selina Hastings, Methodist matriarch and the Countess of Hunting-don, was involved in the lives of two exceptional African Americans: Phillis Wheatley (1753–84) and John Marrant (1755–91). Two significant "firsts" transpired for each person through Lady Huntingdon's support for them. At a time when white Americans would not publish her poems because they doubted Phillis actually wrote them, the countess published Phillis Wheatley's *Poems on Various Subjects Religious and Moral* in London in 1773. Wheatley became the *first* published African-American poet. The publication of her poetry brought Wheatley so much international acclaim that she was, as historian Henry Louis Gates described her, "the most famous African on the face of the earth, the Oprah Winfrey of her time."[11] When John Marrant answered the call to Christian ministry among the black British Loyalists who fled to Nova Scotia after the war of the American Rebellion, he became the *first* African minister formally ordained by a major Protestant body. On May 15, 1785, Lady Huntingdon's Connexion ordained Marrant into full connection and Christian ministry in London, and he preached throughout England that summer prior to embarking for Nova Scotia. But these were *exceptional* black lives whose talent and identification with the white community brought them notoriety, and also distinguished their life experience from that of most black people. It would be a mistake to look at the story black Britons as though these extraordinary lives were at all ordinary.[12] Nor did Lady Huntingdon's support of Wheatley and Marrant directly translate into the uplift or emancipation of others.

The historical amnesia regarding the positive presence of black people in Britain has a sinister underside to it. This was not just a matter of forgetting, or even overlooking people of African descent who really were in "the picture"—as William Hogarth's art demonstrates—it is a matter of ignoring and reshaping their story as a part of a larger project of building the myth of black racial inferiority. The impact of the myth of inferiority upon black life was pernicious and catastrophic because it was a short step from "not-equal" to "not a person." When people of African descent were seen as nonpeople by white Britons, they were treated as property; they were bought, sold, enslaved, and denied basic human rights or citizenship, even when born free.

England began rethinking its attitude toward people of color in the late seventeenth and eighteenth centuries as it began constructing the myth

11. Gates, *Trials of Phillis Wheatley*, 33.

12. Small, "Reconstructing the Black Past," 689–91. Small points out that these "exceptional blacks" were "prominent individuals" who made extraordinary contributions and achieved notoriety, but they did so by because "they were divorced from the black community and were more involved with the white community." In this sense, they do not necessarily represent the life experience and outlook of the average black Briton.

of black inferiority (alongside of its evil twin, white supremacy). Initially, in Tudor England, people of African descent were met with the curiosity and paternalism associated with the "noble savage trope" that emerged in literature like John Dryden's *The Conquest of Granada* (1672) and Thomas Southerne's play, *Oroonoko* (1696).[13] The few blacks who were present were viewed as exotic warriors, culturally foreign, unspoiled by Western civilization, and interesting; they were different, and perhaps naïve or primitive, but not necessarily inferior.

Peter Fryer points to the presence of Coree the Saldanian, a Khoi-khin ("a hottentot" to the Dutch), as a game-changer. Coree had been captured and kidnapped in 1613 by the British East India Company. He was brought to Elizabethan London so the traders could learn about his people for commercial purposes. He was friendly, honest, and loyal—all virtues that were admired in white Christians. In this way, explained Fryer, "Coree's visit to London helped change Europe's image of the Khoi-khin. Instead of being seen as *dangerous* savages, they were seen as strange and mostly *harmless* savages."[14] Ironically, the same virtues that were commendable in a European contributed to the exploitation of Africans.

George Gower, *Elizabeth I, Queen of England and Ireland*, c. 1588, oil on canvas, 97.8 x 72.4 cm, National Portrait Gallery, London. Used with permission.

13. The "noble savage trope" was an idealized depiction of indigenous people which viewed them as examples of unspoiled human nature, people uncorrupted by Western civilization. Most often associated with the writings of Jean-Jacques Rousseau, such as his *Confessions* (1750), *Emile* (1762), or *Dreams of a Solitary Walker* (1776), it predates his work.

14. Fryer, *Staying Power*, 13–14. Emphasis added.

Exploitive social constructs, like white supremacy, sometimes develop subtly, and other times they are as starkly visible as the grotesque "whiteness" popularized by Queen Elizabeth. After narrowly escaping death during a deadly case of small pox in 1562, her appearance became a visible emblem of a mindset that elevated the importance of white complexions and which correspondingly devalued black ones. For elite English ladies, like Elizabeth Tudor, a pallid, white face symbolized youth, virility, wealth, high class, and culture. It showed they were so rich and pampered they did not need to work or even go out-of-doors. When Elizabeth's face was horribly scarred by the pox at the age of twenty-nine, she redoubled her whiteness by slathering on a thick layer of Venetian Ceruse to cover her deep scars. With her flame-red wig and shockingly white face, Elizabeth came "perilously close," writes contemporary fashion critic Inkoo Kang, "to Ronald McDonald cosplay."[15] And her "look" was marketed nearly as broadly as is his. The British monarch's ultra-whiteness was deadly poison in several ways; not only did it reinforce a growing cultural egoism that valued whiteness over blackness, but since Venetian Ceruse was made with white lead it was a poisonous chemical compound that dramatically shortened the lives of stylish women.[16]

When her majesty became "highly discontented to understand that great numbers of negroes and Blackamores . . . are *crept* into this realm," she viewed them as "a great annoyance" and "infidels" and gave an "especial commandment that the said kind of people should be with all speed avoided [banished] and discharged out of this Her Majesty's dominions."[17] However it was that Queen Elizabeth imagined that kidnapped Africans "crept into her realm," she did not want them there. Where people of African descent were wanted, however, was the British Caribbean; there they lived, worked, and died in large numbers while enslaved on the sugar plantations that fed Elizabethan England's sweet tooth and thirst for rum-punch. By 1680, the profitable planters on St. Kitts assured the Lords Trade in London, "It is as great a bondage *for us* to cultivate our plantations without negro slaves as for the Egyptians to make bricks without straw."[18] Verbally playing off a Bible text (Exod 5:18) about Israel's enslavement, the West Indies Company

---

15. Charleston, "Truth Behind Queen Elizabeth's White 'Clown Face' Make Up," para. 24.

16. See Eldridge, *Face Paint*.

17. Unidentified Elizabethan document, quoted in Fryer, *Staying Power*, 12. Emphasis added.

18. West Indies Company report (1677–80), quoted in Fryer, *Staying Power*, 14. Emphasis original.

official did not seem to recognize *he* was playing the role of Pharaoh, the enslaver of God's people and the eventual victim of God's wrath.

As the cultural and racial prejudices against black people took shape in the English-speaking world, the profitability of British colonialism inseparably linked blackness and the inferiority of people of African descent with their enslavement. The shift from "the noble savage" to "happy slave" was a rapid one, and it was as obvious as the difference between Shakespeare's *Othello* (1603), who was a Moorish man of great dignity and complexity, and Mungo, the stereotypical black slave of *The Padlock* (1768). In the popular comedic opera by Isaac Bickerstaff, Mungo was described by Tony Frazier as "lazy, gullible, and untrustworthy, but he possessed a quick wit and lamented his life in servitude."[19]

The prevailing "one great chain of being" philosophy also needs to be taken into account here.[20] It was a short step from the hurtful hierarchy we have observed in ranking the value of social classes, rich and poor—and genders, male and female—to a hierarchical ranking of the races. It was an especially potent tool when the racial trope of the inferiority of black people became a profitable part of Britain's empire-building. The enslavement of West African people was a crucial component of "the triangle trade" that took untold numbers of ships loaded with Africans across the Atlantic to slavery in the New World. In Charleston and elsewhere, ships formerly crammed full of black people unloaded and then were reloaded with agricultural products that were the fruits of their labor. These ships returned to England full of the bounty of colonialism as the raw materials from the Americas fueled the industrial boom of Georgian England. Writing in 1729, British economist Joshua Gee explained the profitability of the British slave trade:

> Our trade with Africa is very profitable to the Nation in general; it has this Advantage, that it carries no Money out, and not only supplies our Plantations with Servants, but brings in a great Deal of Bullion . . . The supplying our Plantations with Negroes is of that extraordinary Advantage to us, that the planting of Sugar and Tobacco, and carrying on Trade there could not be supported without them; which Plantations . . . are the great Causes of the Increase of Riches of the Kingdom.[21]

The theory of black inferiority was also supported by famous philosophers like David Hume (1711–76). In his essay, "Of National Characters" (1753), for example, Hume wrote:

19. Frazier, "Invention of Mungo," 19.
20. McInerney, "Better Sort," 47–53.
21. Gee, *Trade and Navigation of Great-Britain Considered*, 25.

I am apt to suspect the Negroes, and in general all of the other
species of men . . . to be naturally inferior to the whites. There
never was a civilized man of any other complexion than white,
nor even any individual eminent either in action or speculation.
No ingenious manufacturing among them, no arts, no sciences.
. . . In Jamaica, indeed, they talk of one Negro as a man of parts
and learning, but 'tis likely he is admired for very slender accomplishments, like a parrot, who speaks a few works plainly.[22]

While Hume did not speak for all the educated elite, and a few of his contemporaries disagreed with him, there is no ignoring the horribly prejudicial impact of words like these from one who was considered to be a leading
light of the day.[23] Emerging eighteenth-century science, operating in this
same thought-world, presupposed a hierarchy of racial differences and also
verified it.[24]

William Hogarth, *Taste in High Life,* Plate 2, c. 1742, **oil on canvas, 63 x 75 cm,
Metropolitan Museum of Art, New York.**

22. Hume, "Of National Characters," 208.
23. See, for example, Willis, "Impact of David Hume's Thought about Race."
24. Schiesbinger, "Anatomy of Differences."

William Hogarth, *A Rake's Progress, Plate 3,* **1735, engraving, 35.9 x 41.2 cm, Metropolitan Museum of Art, New York. This image is a cropped close-up of the grinning black prostitute in the left background of the original.**

Black Britons are *very* visible in William Hogarth's art of the Georgian period. People of color are seen around the edges of at least five of his pictures of eighteenth-century English life. Hogarth's art also signaled that a major cultural shift was underway with respect to the how black people were viewed. Hogarth's "A Harlot's Progress" (1732), plate 2; "Southwark Fair" (1733); "Taste in High Life" (1742), plate 2; and plate 4 in "Marriage a-la-Mode" (1745), all depict a small black boy (presumably a slave) in exotic attire. Additionally, the pregnant black prostitute in plate 4 of "A Harlot's Progress" signals his willingness to connect the experience of black people with prostitution—metaphorically and otherwise. Art expert Catherine Molineux adds her assessment: "Hogarth's prints undermine—implicitly or not—the idea that mastery over black slaves communicated English virtue and benevolence. His representations of slaves, instead comments on the moral corruption of Londoners who seek to elevate their [own] status."[25]

The formation of the myth of black inferiority was also evident in a racially charged interpretation of the Bible. A racist reading of "the curse of Ham" passage (Gen 9:25) developed in Iberia and appeared in England in the seventeenth century; it soon became standard fare in Georgian England. Noah's curse upon his son, Ham, was interpreted as God's curse of perpetual

25. Molineux, "Hogarth's Fashionable Slaves," 514.

enslavement upon people of African descent. It was an interpretation that conveniently added legitimacy to blacks' enslavement by white culture. This interpretation appeared in English sermons of the seventeenth century, like one by Rev. Robert Wilkenson, who declared that Africans are "the accursed seed of Cham . . . [w]ho had for a stamp [of] their father's sinne, the color of hell set upon their faces."[26] It was buttressed by the findings of nascent cultural anthropologists like George Sandys (1578–1644)[27] and popularized on stage by comedic operas like *Noah's Flood* (1679) by Edward Ecclestone.

Africans generally arrived in England by way of the British Caribbean, often as domestic servants of rich planters or occasionally as runaway slaves. The growing black presence in London soon became a matter of concern to the white populace. In order to discourage black flight to the city, in 1731 the Lord Mayor of London ruled that nonwhites could no longer hold company apprenticeships.[28] Since black people were nonresidents and could not be citizens, they were not eligible for poor relief. Soon a "highly visible group of black men," who were no doubt also homeless, "were forced into beggary, and the 'black poor' became a much-discussed social phenomenon in the final quarter of the eighteenth century."[29] This situation was exacerbated by the arrival of recently discharged black loyalist soldiers fresh from England's wars of empire in North America. They had been promised freedom, land, and a pension for their military service but actually only received "freedom" of a very limited sort.[30] And so racist Britons like Philip Thicknesse, who had recently returned from the Georgia colony, where he had been one of John Wesley's staunchest critics,[31] complained about the double danger he saw in London's growing black presence. Thicknesse feared both violence and the mixing of the races as he wrote: "London abounds with an incredible number of these black men . . . in almost every village are to be seen a little race of mulattoes, mischievous as monkeys and infinitely more dangerous."[32] It is important to view these prejudicial remarks as both a reflection of and contribution to the racial stereotypes developing during this period. In truth, however, only fifty-two people of African descent were charged with crimes in the London courts at that time, and of those only 5.8 percent were charged with violent crime, most of which were associated

---

26. Wilkenson's sermon of 1607, quoted in Goldenberg, *Black and Slave*, 126.

27. Sandys, *Relation of a Journey Begun.*

28. Sandhu, "First Black Britons."

29. Emsley et al., "Black Communities," para. 7.

30. See "Who Were the Black Loyalists?"

31. Blane, "Notes and Documents," 690.

32. Sandhu, "First Black Britons," para. 23.

with theft. Exactly one man, one "Black John," was charged with a sex crime during the entire century.[33]

Were there black Britons among the early English Methodists? Yes. But there is no clear indication as to degree. Extant Methodist class rolls record the occupation and gender of each member (along with their tithe), but not their race. John Wesley's journal, however, preserves a cameo of his encounter with an unnamed black woman he met in the "select Society" (a small group for mature Christians) in Whitehaven. Wesley reported:

> I was particularly pleased with a poor Negro. She seemed to be fuller of love than any of the rest. And not only her voice had an unusual sweetness, but her words were chosen and uttered with a peculiar propriety. I have heard either in England or America such a Negro speaker (man or woman) before.[34]

Of particular importance is the fact that this unnamed black Methodist woman *spoke* in the Methodist Society. This likely means that, according to Methodist custom, she "testified" to what God had done and was doing in her life. It was a dramatically countercultural event on several levels; she was both black *and* a woman speaking at center stage, rather than standing in the background (as in Hogarth's art). John Wesley affirmed this unnamed woman's witness as well as the great effectiveness with which she presented it.

It is very likely that in their early lives, growing up in rural Lincolnshire and attending elite prep schools before going "up to Oxford," the Wesley brothers had almost no contact with black people, and knew almost nothing about black lives. Their missionary trip to Georgia in the American South changed that. In fact, when he first set foot in Georgia, in March 1736, arriving on St. Simons Island, Charles recalled "that remark from Bishop Hall: 'the calling of God never leaves a man unchanged.'"[35] Slavery was illegal in Georgia during the Wesleys' tenure there. But when Charles traveled through Charleston, South Carolina, the citadel of the American slave trade, he was utterly repulsed by what he saw: "I had observed much, and heard more, of the cruelty of masters towards their negroes."[36] After angrily recounting a long list of particulars, Charles Wesley concluded: "It were endless to recount all the shocking instances of diabolical cruelty which these men (as they call themselves) daily practice upon their

33. King and Carter, "Black People and the Criminal Justice System," 112.

34. J. Wesley, *Journal and Diaries* VI:169.

35. C. Wesley, *Manuscript Journal* I:1.

36. C. Wesley, *Manuscript Journal* I:46–47.

fellow-creatures, and that on the most trivial occasions."[37] Moving from shock and outrage to a concern about redress, Charles did not sound hopeful: "These horrid cruelties are the less to be wondered at, because the government itself in effect countenances and allows them to kill their slaves by the ridiculous penalty appointed for it . . . This I can look upon as no other than a public act to indemnify murder."[38] This was one of the first written statements about slavery and black lives extant from the pen of Charles Wesley. It is clear he had already made up his mind about the diabolical nature of slavery.

John Wesley's published journal recorded no angry and emotional outbursts to the barbarity he saw inflicted upon African Americans in the colonies. But when he subsequently attacked slavery in his *Thoughts upon Slavery* (1774), he wrote with credibility: "I speak [about] no more than I know by experience."[39] John accompanied Charles to Charleston in August 1736, and at that point two interrelated behaviors began to emerge in his journal record: Wesley documented the abilities he saw in black people, and he began to minister to them. The first aspect occurred almost subconsciously as John Wesley began to test popular prejudices and stereotypes about people of African descent over against what he was seeing and experiencing—and he consistently found them to be utterly false. This was the Lockean "reasonable" half of Henry Rack's tautology for describing Wesley as the "*Reasonable Enthusiast.*"[40] The Christian "enthusiast" side of him impelled Wesley into ministry with black people. After preaching a Sunday service, for example, John struck up a conversion with a young black woman whose mistress "had many times instructed her in the Christian religion."[41] "I asked her," Wesley reported, "what religion was. She said she could not tell."[42] When she was unable to answer in a way that satisfied him, John did not conclude she *could* not learn, his response was one of compassion and distress about what she did not know and had not yet experienced. "O God," he wrote, "where are thy tender mercies? Are they not over all thy works? When shall the Sun of Righteousness [a Wesleyan euphuism for Jesus Christ] arise on these outcasts of men, with healing in his wings?"[43] Two

---

37. C. Wesley, *Manuscript Journal* I:47.
38. C. Wesley, *Manuscript Journal* I:47.
39. J. Wesley, *Works* XI:73.
40. Rack, *Reasonable Enthusiast.*
41. J. Wesley, *Journal and Diaries* I:169.
42. J. Wesley, *Journal and Diaries* I:169.
43. J. Wesley, *Journal and Diaries* I:169.

weeks later John's private diary reports that he read *The Negro's Advocate.*[44] In that book, Morgan Godwyn argued for "the full liberty of Negroes in the gospel," and attacked the popular interpretation that linked "the Curse of Ham" (Gen 9:25), with black skin color, and the enslavement of African people.[45]

This familiar pattern of observe-and-serve emerged in John's subsequent encounters with African Americans.[46] He found a "Negro lad," with whom Wesley met several times, "both very desirous and very capable on instruction."[47] While his tone sounds condescending from the distance of so many years, it also shows that Wesley was not willing to accept the commonly accepted and often-repeated prejudices about black people. He was assessing and disproving the negative black stereotypes from the standpoint of his own experiences with them, and he reported his positive assessments in his journal. Wesley's resolve, after speaking with the young black man, was to try to devise a plan to "instruct the American Negros in Christianity."[48] Henceforth, support for the instruction and evangelization of people of African descent became a recurrent theme in John Wesley's work.[49] But his own active abolitionism was a journey that came more slowly.[50] It came gradually, perhaps, because active abolitionism required the constitutionally conservative John Wesley to go against his understanding of Christian tradition, a popular interpretation of the Scriptures, and civil law. But in finally taking concerted steps to arrive at active abolitionism, the Wesley brothers traveled a path that other prominent Methodists like George Whitefield[51] and Lady Huntingdon did not; in fact, both of the latter actually wound up owning slaves.[52]

44. J. Wesley, *Journal and Diaries* I:410. This book was *The Negro's and Indians Advocate, Suing for their Admission to the Church, or A Persuasive to the Instructing and Baptizing of the Negro's and Indians in our Plantations Shewing that as the Compliance therewith Can Prejudice No Man's Just Interest, So that the Wilful Neglecting and Opposing of it, Is No Less Than a Manifest Apostacy From the Christian Faith,* by Morgan Godwyn (1680). The title is a fair summary of the contents in the book.

45. See Goldenberg, *Black and Slave.*

46. J. Wesley, *Journal and Diaries* I:180–81.

47. J. Wesley, *Journal and Diaries* I:181.

48. J. Wesley, *Journal and Diaries* I:181.

49. J. Wesley, *Journal and Diaries* I:209; II:435; IV:21–22; 41–42; 84–85; VI:386.

50. Brendlinger, *Social Justice,* plots this development in great detail in "John Wesley's Antislavery Journey," 13–45.

51. See Brendlinger, "Wesley, Whitefield, a Philadelphia Quaker, and Slavery," 164–73.

52. See Tyson, "Lady Huntingdon, Religion, and Race," 32n49.

John Wesley's journey toward active abolitionism can be traced through his correspondence, his preaching, his associations, and his publications. It is evidenced in his *Notes Upon the Old and New Testaments* (1755), for example, which avoided a racist interpretation of the curse of Ham (Gen 9:25).[53] The horribly misused "slaves obey your masters" (Col 3:22), which in the Anglican translation of the A.V. read "servants" instead of "slaves," became, in John Wesley's hands, a call to authentic Christian service with "a simple intention of doing right, without looking any farther."[54] The "man-stealer" of 1 Timothy 1:10 received Wesley's harsh rebuke as "the worst of all thieves, in comparison of whom high-way men and house breakers are innocent!"[55] In his *Doctrine of Original Sin* (1757), Wesley refused to follow one of his main sources, Dr. David Jennings,[56] in a racist interpretation of the curse of Ham passage, and instead John pointed to forced servitude as a prime example of original sin and its horrible impact upon the world.[57]

When the abolitionist movement began in England in the early 1770s, the Wesleys joined the attack upon slavery. They fired off a relentless barrage of anti-slavery sentiments in sermons, tracts, and essays in their *Arminian Magazine*. They also advocated for social change through well-placed letters. They allied themselves with prominent abolitionists like Antony Benezet, Granville Sharp, the brothers Thomas and John Clarkson, Samuel Hoare, and a bit later with William Wilberforce. They may have also met with feminist freedom writer Hannah Moore, who was associated with their literary sister "Patty" Wesley Hall. Moore's abolitionist poem "Slavery" (1788) was published in Wesley's *Arminian Magazine* the moment it was released. And the Wesley brothers became personally involved in the lives of people of African descent.

In February 1772, John Wesley's journal reported that he "read a very different book" published by "an honest Quaker on that execrable sum of all villainies commonly called 'the slave trade.' I read of nothing like it in the heathen world, whether ancient or modern."[58] The book Wesley read was likely *Some Historical Account of Guinea* (1771), by the American abolitionist Antony Benezet (1712–84).[59] It was a consciousness-raising event for

---

53. J. Wesley, *Explanatory Notes* I:42.

54. J. Wesley, *Explanatory Notes* III:523.

55. J. Wesley, *Explanatory Notes* III:538.

56. Jennings, *Vindication of the Scripture-Doctrine of Original Sin.*

57. J. Wesley, *Doctrinal and Controversial Treatises* I:218; cf. 218–45.

58. J. Wesley, *Journal and Diaries* V:307.

59. This was Antony Benezet (1712–84). His *Some Historical Account of Guinea, in Produce, and the General Disposition of its Inhabitants, with an Inquiry into the Rise and Progress of the Slave Trade in its Natures and its Calamitous Effects* (1771) seems to be the book Wesley read.

John Wesley that provided shape and confirmation to experiences he had with black people on both sides of the Atlantic. Benezet and Wesley began a correspondence and became allies in the struggle against slavery.[60] Wesley used Benezet's writings as a main resource for his own abolitionist treatise, *Thoughts upon Slavery* (1774). Benezet wrote him approvingly: "The Tract thou hast lately published entitled, *Thoughts on Slavery*, afforded me much satisfaction." Antony Benezet also republished Wesley's book in Philadelphia, where it became an influential best seller.[61] John Wesley's *Thoughts upon Slavery* was widely read on both sides of the Atlantic, and it went through four editions in just two years.

About the same time he was reading Benezet's book, John Wesley made the acquaintance of Granville Sharp (1735–1813), who was a British civil servant and member of parliament. In 1767, Sharp began earning his reputation as a "defender of the Negro."[62] He also published *A Representation of the Dangerous Tendency of Tolerating Slavery in England* (1769), in which he argued that the laws of nature granted liberty to all people, and any civil law that countermanded the laws of nature was a false law that must be changed. The most significant of Sharp's several legal defense cases was that of the runaway black slave, James Somersett, which came before the King's Bench in the spring of 1772.

The case was about the legality of Somersett's kidnapping and detention in England, for the purpose of returning him to slavery in America. At stake were two, apparently conflicting, rights guaranteed under British common law: the human right to liberty, and the right to own and maintain one's property. Somersett's defenders argued that since he was a person and not an inanimate object or an animal, British common law guaranteed him human liberty. He could not, therefore, be considered to be "property"; the prosecution argued the exact opposite. After much argumentation and deliberation, Lord Mansfield, Charles Wesley's lifelong friend from Charterhouse School days, ruled in favor of James Somersett's freedom: "[W]e cannot say the cause set forth by this return is allowed or approved of by the laws of this kingdom, therefore the man must be discharged."[63]

In a similar case the next spring, two African young men, the brothers Little Ephraim Robin-John and Ancorna Robin-John, runaway slaves from Virginia, were detained by slave hunters while hiding in plain sight

60. Brendlinger, *Social Justice*, 29–30. John Wesley's American correspondent was unnamed, but Antony Benezet seems like the obvious person.

61. *Brendlinger, Social* Justice, 178–79.

62. See Gerzina, *Black London*, 90–133, for an illuminating presentation of this case.

63. Quoted in Thomas, "Case of Somersett," para. 13.

in Bristol, England. Granville Sharpe brought their case before Justice Lord Mansfield, who provided a warrant for their release. While the Robin-John brothers were staying in Bristol, they were befriended and ministered to by Charles Wesley. John Wesley subsequently published a narrative account of the Robin-John case in *Arminian Magazine* in 1783: "While they were at Bristol," he wrote, "Mr. Charles Wesley was desired to visit them. From that time they came to him every day. He taught them to read, and carefully instructed them in the principles of Christianity."[64]

These events led up to the publication of John Wesley's *Thoughts upon Slavery* in the spring of 1774. As Wesley presented his case against slavery, four very significant matters were apparent in his argument. First, "the African is in *no respect inferior* to the European," he wrote. "Their stupidity, therefore, in our plantations is not natural; otherwise than it is the natural effect of their condition. Consequently, it is *not their* fault, but *yours*: you [the reader] must answer for it, before God and man."[65] So much for the myth of inherent black inferiority! Wesley knew from personal experience it was a lie, and he set about to tell the whole world the whole truth. Secondly, "Liberty is the right of every human creature, as soon as he breathes the vital air; and no human law can deprive him of that right which he derives from the law of nature."[66] The implications of this principle were both obvious and far-reaching:

> If therefore, you have any regard to justice (to say nothing of mercy, nor the revealed law of God), render unto all their due. Give liberty to whom liberty is due, that is, to every child of man, to every partaker of human nature. Let none serve you but by his own act and deed, by his own voluntary choice. Away with all whips, all chains, all compulsion! Be gentle towards all men; and see that you invariably do unto everyone as you would he should do unto you.[67]

Wesley asserted that people of African descent must be treated as *people*, not as property, and on that basis Jesus' "golden rule"—"do unto others as you would have others do unto you" (Matt 7:12)—applied to black people, and it applied to the issue of slavery.

Third, John Wesley would not allow it to be said that the British slave trade was as benevolent and paternalistic as others often described it, as

---

64. J. Wesley, *Arminian Magazine*, May 23, 1787, quoted in Brendlinger, *Social Justice*, 176.

65. J. Wesley, *Works* XI:74. Emphasis original.

66. J. Wesley, *Works* XI:79.

67. J. Wesley, *Works* XI:79.

though it was a situation which had mutual benefits for slave and master. He reported the inhumanity and brutality of the slave trade (with the help of Benezet's material) from beginning to end. There was absolutely no benevolence about it at all. Wesley depicted it as sub-Christian and subhuman behavior. And as surely as God judged Sodom and Gomorrah, he predicted, God would be coming in judgment again: "There must be a state of retribution; a state wherein the just God will reward every man according to his works. Then what reward will he render to you? . . . O think now, 'He shall have judgment without mercy that showed no mercy.'"[68]

And finally, there was so much guilt and blame associated with the slave trade that it touched everyone; no one was innocent, Wesley argued. From the person who stole African people from their homes, to the captain who transported them, those who sold and those who bought them, as well as those who benefited from the extorted labor of brutalized slaves, all were guilty; there was guilt enough for everyone to have their share. But why does this inhumanity happen? It was all about the money. Mouthing the claims of his opponents, who reported that "furnishing us with slaves is necessary for the trade, and wealth, and glory, of our nation,"[69] John Wesley reacted strongly to the phrases "necessary" and "glory of our nation" as he asserted: "Wealth is *not* necessary to the glory of our nation; but wisdom, virtue, justice, mercy, generosity, public spirit love of country. *These* are necessary to the real *glory* of a nation; but the abundance of wealth is not."[70] He concluded, "Better *no* trade, than trade procured by villainy. It is far better to have no wealth, than to gain wealth at the expense of virtue. Better is honest poverty, than all the riches bought by the tears, and sweat, and blood, of our fellow-creatures."[71] John Wesley understood and denounced chattel slavery for what it was: a tool of British colonialism and empire-building, a money-making scheme, and an institution rooted in greed, materialism, and violence. Slavery was fueled by human self-centeredness and greed, and therefore it was utterly based in sin.

As Georgian England reeled under severe scarcity and economic decline, due in large part to Britain's wars of empire, John Wesley wrote several stinging socioeconomic critiques of his homeland. He placed the blame of the nation's ruin directly in Britain's own blood-stained hands:

> As we are punished with the sword, it is not improbable but one principal sin of our nation is, the blood that we have shed in

68. J. Wesley, *Works* XI:77.
69. J. Wesley, *Works* XI:73.
70. J. Wesley, *Works* XI:73. Emphasis original.
71. J. Wesley, *Works* XI:73–74. Emphasis original.

Asia, Africa, and America. Here I would beg your serious attention, while I observe, that however extensively pursued, and of
long continuance the African [slave] trade may be, it is never-
theless iniquitous from first to last. It is the price of blood! It is a
trade of blood, and has stained our land with blood.[72]

Unfortunately, none of the Wesley brothers' sermons against slavery
have survived, largely because they often preached *ex tempore* (as they described it), without notes. John's journal reported at least one instance, in
March 1777, when he went into a citadel of slave trade to preach against it.[73]
Charles Wesley also attacked slavery in his hymns and poems. In "On the
Slave Trade," for example, Charles's poetic voice spoke as an African who
pointed out that if white Britons were not "slaves to gold," then Africans
would not be slaves at all:

Deem our nations brutes no longer,
Till some reason ye shall find,
Worthier of regard and stronger,
Than the colors of your kind,
Slaves of gold, whose sordid dealings
Tarnish all your boasted pow'rs,
Prove that ye have human feelings
Ere ye proudly question ours.[74]

When the "Society for Effecting the Abolition of the Slave Trade" was
established in London on May 22, 1787, the movement received the Wesleys' full support. John wrote to Granville Sharp, "Ever since I heard of it first
I felt a perfect detestation of the horrid Slave Trade, but more particularly
since I had the pleasure of reading what you have published upon the subject. Therefore I cannot but do everything in my power to forward the glori-
ous design of your Society."[75] The aged Wesley put the weight of his moral
authority behind the abolitionist movement, so long as he had life. Less
than a month before his death, John Wesley wrote parliamentarian William
Wilberforce what would turn out to be Wesley's last letter, and his last abolitionist effort, in February 1791.[76] He depicted Wilberforce as a modern-day

72. J. Wesley, *Works* XI:125. See also *Address to the People of England, With Regard
to the State of the Nation* (1778).

73. J. Wesley, *Journal and Diaries* VI:46.

74. J. Wesley, *Arminian Magazine*, March 1788, quoted in Brendlinger, *Social Justice*, 39–41.

75. J. Wesley, *Letters* VIII:17.

76. Willam Wilberfoce (1759–1833), from a religious standpoint, was an Anglican
evangelical whose family had been impacted by the ministry of Methodist evangelist

Athanasius who alone "stood against the world" by standing against slavery. Once again, John Wesley described slavery as "that exercrable villany which is the scandal of religion, of England, and of human nature."[77] John prayerfully encouraged Wilberforce: "But if God be for you, who can be against you? Be not weary of well doing! Go on, in the name of God, and in the power of His might, till even American slavery (the vilest that ever saw the sun) shall vanish away before it."[78] Wesley seemed a bit prophetic in his letter to William Wilberforce because two months later, when Wilberforce's antislavery bill came to a vote in the House of Commons, it was soundly defeated by a vote of 163 to 88. But through the continued efforts of Wilberforce and others, the Slave Trade Act, which outlawed slavery in Britain, was finally passed in 1807. The Abolition Act of 1833, enacted exactly three days before William Wilberforce's death, abolished the slave trade throughout all British dominions.

The early Methodists welcomed black Britons into the counterculture of Methodist bands and Societies where the familial language of "sister" and "brother" was preferred to the phrases of hierarchy and racial prejudice. Methodism became a place where black lives mattered. Charles Wesley responded to racism viscerally and spontaneously; he knew in his heart it was deeply wrong. John Wesley responded more cognitively and strategically, but they both responded. The Wesleys and their colleagues tried to deconstruct the myth of black racial inferiority and mounted a concerted campaign for the full liberty of people of African descent. But the dilemma of race and the slavery situation in America was even more villainous than in their mother country. Methodism's struggle with America's "original sin" of racism was a long and painful one (cf. chapter 16).

QUESTIONS FOR FURTHER CONSIDERATION:

1. What do you do when an interpretation of Scripture or Christian tradition hinders, rather than helps to produce, acceptance, inclusion, and justice in your world?

2. Are you aware of how subtly hurtful racial and other stereotypes can be constructed in your mind and our society? What steps can you take to guard against this development?

George Whitefiield, though he drifted away from and then returned to vital piety. His acquaintance with John Newton (1725–1807), former slaver-turned-abolitionist and composer of "Amazing Grace" (1779), influenced Wilberforce's crusade against slavery.

77. J. Wesley, *Letters* VIII:265.
78. J. Wesley, *Letters* VIII:265.

3. When you encounter hurtful attitudes, stereotypes, and racial prejudice in your faith community, or elsewhere, what can you do about it?

4. Are you willing to examine your own attitudes, expressions, programs,
   and associations to ascertain whether they are indeed welcoming towards people of all races?

5. What practical steps can you take towards achieving greater acceptance and racial inclusion at all levels of your life? In our lives together
   as a community?

CHAPTER 9

"Just Enough Religion to Make Us Hate"

The Crisis Caused by Religious Prejudice

"WE HAVE JUST ENOUGH religion to make us *hate*, but not enough to make us *love one another*," wrote Jonathan Swift, the author of *Gulliver's Travels*, in 1711.[1] As an Irish-born, English-educated (MA, Oxford, 1692) Anglican Bishop in Dublin, Ireland, (1712–45) Swift had seen and experienced enough religious intolerance to write about it like an expert. On a practical level, the practice of Roman Catholicism was illegal in England for 232 years from the Elizabethan Act of Uniformity (1558) until 1791, when Roman Catholic Britons were finally granted civil rights.[2] It was a prime example of institutionalized prejudice and discrimination.

The history of distrust and animosity between Protestants (Anglicans and otherwise) and Roman Catholics in England reached back to the sixteenth-century Reformation. It was kept alive, in part, by the popularity of Fox's *Book of Martyrs*, which painted Roman Catholicism as a brutal and subversive faith intent upon world domination by the pope. The *Book of Martyrs* fueled the florid descriptions of Protestant martyrs that lived on in the sermons of popular eighteenth-century preachers like Thomas Baldwin.[3] Religious tests for political life, higher education, and important vocations made life difficult for Roman Catholic Britons, who made up over 2 percent of the population in the Georgian era. Punitive acts and

1. Swift, *Miscellanies*, 233. Emphasis original.
2. See "Penal Laws Against English Catholics," in Butler, *Methodists and Papists*, 205–10.
3. Abbott, "Clerical Responses to the Jacobite Rebellion in 1715," 338.

public antipathy caused the English Roman Catholic gentry, called "the recusants," to withdraw to their country estates where they cultivated a Jacobite counterculture.

Fear and distrust of, as well as hatred against, Catholics increased dramatically because of Jacobite invasions that shook England in 1715, and again in 1745. John Wesley evidenced the broad impact of the "anti-Catholic paranoia" of the mid-1740s when he penned "An Address to the King," which distanced the Methodists from Roman Catholicism and pledged their loyalty to the Church and Crown; but then "upon farther consideration it was judged best to lay it aside."[4] The "further consideration" was a strongly worded letter from his brother, Charles, contesting the idea.[5] Later that same year, John's sermon "Scriptural Christianity," preached "at St. Mary's Oxford before the University" on August 24, 1744, closed by warning Anglicans that if they did not reform themselves, God would send judgment upon them: "Whom then shall God send? The famine, the pestilence (the last messengers of God to a guilty land), or the sword? The armies of the Romish 'aliens,' to reform us into our first love [i.e., Roman Catholicism]."[6] Like the "four horsemen of the apocalypse" (Rev 6:1–8), religious prejudice was a harbinger of divine judgment and destruction.

British animosity against Roman Catholicism ran so deep in Georgian culture that "the Jesuit" became a standard symbol for "the devil" in gothic novels of the period.[7] Entire sets of one-pint beer mugs were tastefully decorated with visceral anti-Catholic art and slogans, signaling, as Danielle Thom points out, that the "phenomenon of British anti-Catholicism was not purely sectarian or religiously informed, but intersected with questions of national identity, gender, class and consumption."[8] Muscular anti-Catholicism was as much a political apology for the Hanoverian dynasty as it was an emblem of the beer-drinking crowd of lower-class workers who associated Roman Catholic faith with the effeminate and lavish lifestyle they saw in the recusant gentry.[9]

The Wesley brothers had little direct contact with Roman Catholicism in their early lives. But their roots in the Anglican High Church tradition led more austere Protestants to believe that the Wesleys *were* Roman Catholics. It is well documented that both brothers read numerous Roman Catholic

---

4. J. Wesley, *Journal and Diaries* III:17.

5. C. Wesley, *Manuscript Journal* II:392.

6. J. Wesley, *Sermons* I:179–80.

7. Hoeveler, "Anti-Catholicism and the Gothic Imagery," 2–6.

8. Thom, "Sawney's Defence," para. 3.

9. Haynes, "Culture of Judgment," 483–505.

spiritual writers with great appreciation,[10] and John Wesley's fifty-volume *Christian Library: Extracts from and Abridgments of the Choicest Pieces of Practical Divinity Which Have Been Published in the English Tongue* included selections from many Roman Catholic devotional writers.[11] Most of the Wesleys' early writings about Catholicism showed them trying to distinguish themselves from "the Papists" at a time when that association was both derogatory and dangerous. After several months of verbal and physical abuse from angry mobs, during his initial months of evangelism *alfresco,* John Wesley intimated: "the report now current in Bristol was that I was 'a Papist, if not a Jesuit.' Some added that I was 'born and bred at Rome,' which many cordially believed."[12] Even more frustrating than this falsehood, in John's view, was the fact that his listeners could not distinguish his proclamation of reconciliation with God through faith in Jesus Christ alone, and the message of Roman Catholicism. He lamented this perceived error in this journal as "the most destructive of all those errors which Rome, the mother of abominations . . . [advocates] that *we are justified by works* or (to express the same thing a little more decently) by faith *and* works."[13] Charles Wesley shared a similar view, opining that the "worst error of Popery" was "justification by Works."[14] John's published journal included a letter he wrote to a Roman Catholic correspondent, probably in the summer of 1735, in which he stated:

> I can by no means approve the scurrility and contempt with which the Romanists have often been treated. I dare not rail at or despise any man, much less those who profess to believe in the same Master. But I pity them much, having the same assurance that Jesus is the Christ and that *no* Romanist can expect to be saved according to the terms of His covenant.[15]

John's detailed letter marked out a theological line of demarcation between Methodists and Roman Catholics, largely because he believed the Catholics mistakenly added ten religious obligations to the plain message of the Scriptures.[16]

10. Berger, "Charles Wesley and Roman Catholicism," 208.

11. J. Wesley's original fifty volumes were reduced to thirty in the edition found in the bibliography.

12. J. Wesley, *Journal and Diaries* II:89.

13. J. Wesley, *Journal and Diaries* II:89. Emphasis original.

14. Tyson "Charles Wesley, Evangelist," 49.

15. J. Wesley, *Journal and Diaries* II:91. Emphasis original.

16. J. Wesley, *Journal and Diaries* II:92.

The disinformation campaign about the Wesleys' Catholicism continued intermittently throughout the first few decades of their ministry and was often accompanied by mob violence against them. In Wednesbury, Staffordshire, for example, "Riotous mobs were summoned together by sound of a horn; men, women, and children abused in the most shocking manner; being beaten, stoned, covered with mud; some, even pregnant women, treated in a manner that cannot be mentioned."[17] Apparently, hunting Methodists to the sound of the horn was nearly as much sport as a fox hunt! The whispering campaign about the Methodists' Popery was supplemented by published attacks substantive enough that John Wesley felt the need to answer them in his *Earnest Appeal to Men of Reason and Religion* (1743).[18] The attacks by Anglican Bishop of Exeter, George Lavington, were immensely popular and, coming as they did in the midst of rising political ire against the Roman Catholics, were dangerous.[19]

At the same time John Wesley was refuting claims that he and the Methodists were closet Papists, he was privately moving toward a more irenic assessment of Roman Catholicism. His open letter of 1739 stated "no Romanist can expect to be saved,"[20] but by 1745, "the narrow gate" that leads to salvation had been opened wide enough—in his mind, at least—to allow a few of his favorite Roman Catholic writers, like Thomas à Kempis and Francis de Sales, to get in.[21] By 1750, his writings indicate that John Wesley believed that God worked capably through Roman Catholics and to say otherwise made a person a religious bigot.

In his sermon "A Caution Against Bigotry," based on Mark 9:38–39—"Master, we saw one casting out devils in thy name, and we forbade him, because he followeth not us"—John Wesley borrowed and then rephrased the text's fundamental question: "What if I were to see *a Papist*, an Arian, a Socinian casting out devils?" Answering himself, Wesley wrote: "If I did, I could not forbid even him without convicting myself of bigotry . . . And not only [should we] acknowledge but rejoice in his work, and praise his name with thanksgiving."[22] The irenic and pragmatic side John Wesley surfaced, as he said in effect, if we see that God is working through people not of our own party, those "who foillow us not," even "a Papist,"

---

17. J. Wesley, *Works* XIII:311.

18. J. Wesley, *Appeals to Men of Reason and Religion*, 74–77.

19. Lavington, *Enthusiasm of Methodists and Papists Comp'd*.

20. J. Wesley, *Journal and Diaries* II:89.

21. J. Wesley, *Journal and Diaries* II:89.

22. J. Wesley, *Sermons* II:77. Emphasis original.

rather than condemning them like a religious bigot we should rejoice that God is still working in our world.

In August of 1745 the second Jacobite rebellion began in the Scottish Highlands as Charles Edward Stuart's army made its way south towards London to seize the English throne that "Bonnie Prince Charlie" believed was rightfully his own. All of this was unknown to John Wesley as he made his summer preaching tour through Cornwall and Wales, and then headed north towards Newcastle. The further north Wesley pushed his evangelism, the harsher became the mob violence he met. In St. Ives, a mob burst open the door of the preaching house and tried to grab Wesley for impressment into military service. At Falmouth, an angry mob burst into the Society Room while John was preaching and he was fortunate to escape unharmed. At Tolcarn, Wesley was met at the edge of town by a delegation from the Methodist Society who begged him to go no further lest he be harmed, arrested, or worse. One person took John Wesley aside and confided: "Sir, I will tell you the ground of this. All the gentlemen of these parts say that you have been a long time in France and Spain and are now sent hither by the Pretender, and that these societies are to join him."[23] It was not the first time, nor would it be the last, that possessors of wealth and power turned religious prejudice to their own advantage.

By the time John Wesley reached Newcastle on September 18, 1745, preparations were underway for a Jacobite assault that never came. When Wesley felt it inappropriate for him to attend the city's civil defense meeting, tensions were so high that he needed to write a letter of apology to the Mayor to explain his absence and to pledge his loyalty to the Crown.[24] John carried out his ministry while battlements were thrown up, a cannon placed at the city gates, and a citizen militia conscripted and drilled; a purported spy was interrogated to death. The rebel army was sighted seventeen miles west of Newcastle, on October 5, but it did not attack, and John Wesley continued a fruitful ministry to the terrified citizens. Charles Wesley ministered in Bristol during the autumn invasion and his ministry was also impacted by it, though less directly.[25] At that time, Charles wrote and subsequently published six long *Hymns for Times of Trouble* that communicated his reaction to the Jacobite invasion:

> The waster of Rome Is now on his way,
> The lion is come To scatter and slay;
> Beyond his fierce power We run to the Lamb,

23. J. Wesley, *Journal and Diaries* III:78.
24. J. Wesley, *Journal and Diaries* III:91.
25. C. Wesley, *Manuscript Journal* II:448.

And rest in the tower of Jesus' name.[26]

Religious prejudice was also a continuing theme and challenge during the Methodist evangelistic mission to Roman Catholic Ireland. The Wesleys' work in Ireland began in 1747; it was soon enough after the Jacobite rebellion that the timing gives one pause: Did they interpret the religiopolitical conflict as a call from God? Perhaps they did!

Ireland was England's first colony with a British presence there since the Norman Conquest, but it was Elizabeth I who began the colonization of Ireland in earnest in order to incorporate it into the larger project of Britannia.[27] In 1609, James I began the Ulster Plantation, which settled English-speaking Protestants into Northern Ireland to further its colonization. English, Protestant gentry were granted large tracts of land, and ruled over the rural Irish Catholic peasants in a blatant attempt to "civilize" the region by stamping out Gaelic culture, language, and Irish Roman Catholicism.[28] Under that arrangement, Irish Roman Catholics—who comprised more than 75 percent of the population—owned less than 14 percent of the land, and were systematically excluded from the ownership of farms or businesses.[29] British control of the Irish agricultural economy turned it into a client state of England that could only sell Irish goods in British markets, at British prices. The Royal Navy was stationed at Cork and conscripted almost all of the Irish beef and salt pork at cut-rate prices. Peter King, Anglican Archbishop of Dublin, described the impact of these events to a British correspondent in 1713: "One half of the year people in Ireland eat neither bread nor flesh nor wear Shoes or Stockings; your Hoggs in England and Essex Calves lie and live better than they." Seven years later, Peter King reported: "The cry of the whole people is loud for bread, God knows what will be the consequence, many are starved and I am afraid many more will."[30] Bishop King was right; when a poor harvest was followed by an exceptionally cold winter in 1740–41, more than 400,000 Irish people died.[31]

The impact of so many Irish people having no opportunity for employment or education, and the resultant widespread poverty, hunger, and hopelessness, created a context in which Anglophone racial stereotypes about the inferiority of ignorant, lazy, and drunken Irish Catholics were easily formed and widely popularized. Bishop Jonathan Swift, serving in Dublin at the

26. C. Wesley and J. Wesley, *Poetical Works* IV:89.

27. Canny, "Ideology of English Colonization," 575–98.

28. Magennis, "Present State of Ireland," 594.

29. Lein, "Jonathan Swift and the Population of Ireland," 431–53.

30. R. O'Brien, *Studies in the History of Ireland*, 335.

31. G. O'Brien, *Economic History of Ireland*, 105–6.

time, offered a more plausible explanation: "We are apt to charge the Irish with laziness, because we seldom find them employed; but then we don't consider they have nothing to do."[32] Under such harsh social conditions, a strong British military presence in Ireland was needed to maintain colonial control. They carved out a strip of land, centered in Dublin, that stretched from Dundalk in Louth to Bray in Wicklow, called "the Pale" (stemming from an Old English term for a "picket fence"). It was the base of English political and military rule.[33]

John Wesley offered no specific explanation for expanding Method-ism's evangelistic work into Ireland; perhaps his personal rendition of the "Great Commission" (Matt 28:16–20) was reason enough: "I look upon all the world as my parish; thus far I mean, that in whatever part of it I am, I judge it . . . my bounden duty to declare unto all that are willing to hear the glad tidings of salvation. This is the work which I know God has called me to."[34] His first evangelistic tour began in August 1747, and over the course of nearly fifty years, John visited Ireland for evangelism another twenty-one times. Charles Wesley arrived soon after John left, on September 8, 1747, and stayed until the following March. Initially, John Wesley did not "go be-yond the Pale," which meant, whether he intended it or not, "his mission worked downward from the gentry class and outward from the garrison in a way that would have been unthinkable in England."[35] This approach aligned John Wesley's work so closely with the British colonizers that his ministry among the Roman Catholic peasantry was impeded. Wesley seemed naively surprised when very few Irish people visited him at his lodgings in the Pale. But he saw and heard enough to be mildly critical of the Anglican mission in Ireland: "Is it any wonder that those who are born Papists generally live and die such, when the Protestants can find no better ways to convert them than penal laws and Acts of Parliament?"[36]

Planting Methodism in Ireland took far more tenacity than it did in the Wesleys' native England, and the harvest was much more meager. When they preached out of doors, beyond the bounds of the English Pale, they faced congregations that were often more like lynch mobs. On several occa-sions, it was only the intervention of British soldiers that saved them from serious bodily harm, if not worse. Those young men, far from home and in hostile territory, became a fertile field for Wesleyan evangelism. The same

32. Swift, "Present Miserable State of Conditions in Ireland," 7:164.

33. *Oxford Reference Dictionary*, s.v. "Pale."

34. J. Wesley, *Journal and Diaries* II:69.

35. J. Wesley, *Journal and Diaries* I:56.

36. J.Wesley, *Journal and Diaries* III:189.

was true for other "unassimilated Protestants," like the French Huguenots
and German Palatines, who had fled their homelands because of religious
persecution, only to find themselves amidst the boiling religious resentment
between Protestants and Roman Catholics in Ireland. "These people," John
Wesley thought, "have quite a different look from the natives of the country,
as well as a different temper. They are a serious, thinking people. And their
diligence turns all their land into a garden."[37]

Whether or not Wesley was affected by the racial stereotypes circulating among the English about the Irish (the editors of Wesley's journal think
not[38]), the contrast he drew between the "shanty Irish" and serious, thinking, and diligent Protestants from Europe suggests otherwise. On those few
occasions when Wesley met with the proper "Britishness" he expected to
find throughout Ireland, he paused to celebrate it: "We . . . went through
miserable roads to Coleraine, but the company there made amends for
them. We met with a *right English* society in spirit, in carriage, and even
in dress."[39] Irish Catholic nationals, by contrast, John Wesley found to be
"indolent" and "fickle." And, "He was driven almost speechless by the tendency to exaggerate and the 'pompous accounts' of even the Methodists; his
reaction to the level of truthfulness of the rest may be imagined."[40] Wesley's
disdain for the Irish and their culture was thinly veiled.

As Anglophones and well-educated Anglican clergy, the Wesley brothers looked, to Irish Catholic peasants, like the face of British colonialism.
John Wesley in particular did not readily appreciate the depth of Ireland's
"national problem." He saw the horrific treatment that the poor Irish people
received and complained about it to his journal, on one occasion. He ac-
cidently became aware of Irish political radicalism when he suddenly came
face to face with an Irish republican vigilante group called "the Whiteboys."
They looked like an Irish version of the KKK, wearing "white cockades and
white linen frocks"[41] to mete out clandestine retribution upon Irish people
they deemed to be too cooperative with the British.

John Wesley developed a strategy for evangelizing Roman Catholic
listeners, which he published in 1752 as *A Short Method of Converting all
the Roman Catholics in the Kingdom of Ireland.* His "short method" was to
bypass both the authority of the local priests and the church they represented to speak directly to the people about "the faith of the holy Apostles,"

---

37. J. Wesley, *Journal and Diaries* I:368.

38. J. Wesley, *Journal and Diaries* I:74.

39. J. Wesley, *Journal and Diaries* VII:139. Emphasis added.

40. J. Wesley, *Journal and Diaries* I:74.

41. J. Wesley, *Journal and Diaries* IV:369.

"since they prefer the Apostles before their own Clergy."[42] What should be preached, John Wesley urged, was not only the apostles' deeds, but "their *inward* life . . . [how] they 'lived the life which is hid with Christ in God.'"[43] Charles had already worked out his own "short method" for converting Roman Catholics by building common ground with them. When he addressed a large crowd on the village green in Newgate, Ireland, for example, Charles Wesley preached:

> Come unto me, all ye that are weary' [Matt 11:28]. His [Christ's] power was upon the hearers, keeping down all opposition. I spoke with great freedom to the poor Papists, urging them to repentance and the love of Christ, from the authority of their own Kempis, and their own liturgy. None lifted up his voice or hand. All listened with strange attention. Many were in tears. I advised them to go to their respective places of worship. They expressed general satisfaction, especially the Papists. This also God wrought.[44]

The Wesleys found most of their Irish Methodist adherents among the transplanted Protestants in Ireland, some of whom would eventually carry their Methodism with them to North America. At least five Methodist Societies were established in Dublin, and a few others were scattered throughout the countryside. Among their most notable Irish converts were the former Roman Catholic Thomas Walsh (1730–59) and Adam Clarke (1762–1832), a former Presbyterian. Walsh became an ardent evangelist and trusted associate of the Wesleys, and Clarke became one of early Methodism's most able theologians. But in truth, Methodism was generally seen as an Anglian (Church of Ireland) movement and did not flourish beyond the Pale in Roman Catholic Ireland until after 1799, when Irishmen Gideon Ouseley, Charles Graham, and James McQuigg were commissioned by the Methodist Conference and authorized to preach to the Irish in Gaelic.

In 1749, anti-Methodist riots broke out in Cork, Ireland, during which one popular slogan was "five pounds for a Swadler's [Methodist's] head."[45] In response to this religious hostility, John Wesley penned a remarkably conciliatory *Letter to a Roman Catholic*. He acknowledged that false tales, on both sides, had made it difficult for them to follow

---

42. J.Wesley, *Journal and Diaries* IV:130.

43. J. Wesley, *Journal and Diaries* IV:130–31. Emphasis original.

44. C. Wesley, *Manuscript Journal* II:509.

45. On the nickname "Swadler," see Charles Wesley's journal entry for September 10, 1747, in C. Wesley, *Manuscript Journal* II:506–7.

our Lord's rule, 'Judge not, that ye be not judged'; and [this] has many ill consequences . . . we are on both sides less willing to help one another, and are more ready to hurt each other. Hence, brotherly love is utterly destroyed; and each side, looking on the other side as monsters, gives way to anger, hatred, malice, and every unkind affection . . .[46]

Or to borrow the words of Bishop Jonathan Swift, we "have just enough religion to make us *hate*, but not enough to makes us *love one another*."[47] Wesley admitted to the Catholic reader: "I do not suppose all the bitterness is on your side. I know there is too much on our side also; so much, that I fear many Protestants (so called) will be angry at me too, for writing you in this manner."[48] Wesley sought "to remove in some measure the ground of your unkindness, by plainly declaring what our belief and what our practice is; that you may see, we are not altogether such monsters as perhaps you imagined us to be."[49] Wesley offered a summary of the beliefs of "a true Protestant" which followed the outline of the Apostles' Creed, but curiously added the perpetual virginity of Mary, "the blessed Virgin Mary, who, as well as after as before she brought him forth, continued a pure and unspotted virgin."[50] On other matters, John Wesley suggested, "We will not now enter into dispute."[51] As helpful as John Wesley's overtures towards Roman Catholics may have been on a theological or spiritual level, he did not recognize their legitimate grievances, nor did he address the degree to which his own national Church was complicit in the suffering of the Irish Roman Catholic people; hence, he offered no plan for relief or redress.

The British people's war in America brought significant turmoil to England and in ways that directly affected Roman Catholics. In 1778, through the instigation of Edmund Burke and others,[52] Parliament passed the Papists Act of 1778—also called the Catholic Relief Act. The Act granted limited civil liberties to Roman Catholics by repealing portions of the harsh, century-old Act by the same name (1698). Capitalizing upon the religious tolerance of "the Age of Reason," the Papist Act of 1778 was really about paving the way for Roman Catholics, notably from the Scottish Highlands and Ireland, to serve in the British military. Appearing as it did just two

---

46. J. Wesley, *Works* X:80.

47. Swift, *Miscellanies*, 233. Emphasis original.

48. J. Wesley, *Works* X:80

49. J. Wesley, *Works* X:81.

50. J. Wesley, *Works* X:81.

51. J. Wesley, *Works* X:82.

52. P. Walsh, "New Edmund Burke Letter," 159–63.

months after the signing of the Franco-American alliance for the war in America, it attempted to offset the potential influx of French military manpower with Roman Catholics from Great Britain.[53] Prime Minster North hoped the new Papist Act would be well received and easily implemented on humanitarian grounds, but he was sorely disappointed. In 1779, organized opposition emerged through the efforts of Lord George Gordon (1751–93), who, with several prominent Protestant Calvinist ministers, including Erasmus Middleton and Rowland Hill, formed the Protestant Association of London with the express intention of repealing the Catholic Relief Act. Their motivation was pure anti-Catholic prejudice, fueled by xenophobia.

John Wesley's irenic attitude towards Roman Catholics had evaporated by the time he published *Popery Calmly Considered* in 1779. Popular opposition to the Catholic Relief Act was fierce. In this politically volatile situation, there was really nothing "calm" about John Wesley's treatise, despite its title.[54] It not only stirred up old prejudices and undermined public trust in Roman Catholics, but by strongly opposing the Catholic Relief Act in prejudicial terms, Wesley's *Popery Calmly Considered* directly contributed to the volatile situation that led to the bloody Gordon Riots.

While there is no direct evidence that John Wesley joined the anti-Catholic Protestant Association, he certainly aided their cause through his publications. His open letter "To the Printer of the Public Advisor, Occasioned by the Late Act Passed in Favor of Popery," was published in the newspaper on January 12, 1780. In it, John disowned active Catholic persecution: "With persecution I have nothing to do. I persecute no man for his religious principles . . . But this does not touch the point."[55] "The point," was, however, that all Roman Catholics should be viewed as potential terrorists, and Wesley referred again to the arcane statement from the Council of Constance as his evidence. If it is difficult for the modern reader to imagine the harmful impact of Wesley's rhetoric, we need only recall the reaction of segments of the American populace to the presence of Muslims in their midst following 9/11. While John wound up siding with religious prejudice and exclusion instead of "catholic love," Charles Wesley's assessment of the Protestant Association and their aims was quite different. He published a hymnological lampoon of the Protestant Association, ridiculing them as a band of mixed-up misfits and misguided zealots, "an army of Associates/Of rebels, regicides, and traitors."[56]

---

53. Donovan, "Military Origins of the Roman Catholic Relief Programme," 79–102.
54. J. Wesley, *Works* X:157.
55. J. Wesley, *Letters* VI:371.
56. C. Wesley and J. Wesley, *Poetical Works* VIII:450.

The Gordon Riots have been described as the "most violent riots in London's long and turbulent history"; the five days of mob violence "brought the capital of Britain's immense empire to a near standstill."[57]

John Seymour Lucas, *The Gordon Riots*, 1879, oil on canvas, Art Gallery of New South Wales, from Project Gutenberg.

"In the process, at least 450 Londoners and 210 soldiers lost their lives and numerous city shops, homes, government offices, chapels, and prisons lay in ashes."[58] More than 500 rioters were arrested, including Lord Gordon himself.[59] John Wesley did not witness the riots, but Charles Wesley did. He urged his brother:

> Imagine the terror of the poor papists. I prayed with the preachers at the Chapel, and charged them to keep the peace. I preached peace and charity, the one true religion, and prayed earnestly for the trembling, persecuted Catholics. Never have I found such love for them as on this occasion. I believe most of the Society are like minded.[60]

Charles's less ideological and more compassionate response was also more theologically sound than John's. And Charles Wesley's *Hymns in the Time of the Tumults* left a clear statement of what he thought about the Gordon

57. Jones, "'In Favour of Popery,'" 79.
58. C. Wesley and J. Wesley, *Poetical Works* VIII:82.
59. Jones, "'In Favor of Popery,'" 79–82.
60. C. Wesley, quoted in Jackson, *Life of Charles Wesley*, 677.

Riots: "As in religion's cause they join,/And blasphemously call it Thine [God's]/The cause of persecuting zeal,/Of treason, anarchy, and hell."[61]

"On Roman Catholicism," noted Henry Rack, "[John] Wesley was . . . equivocal; he was more bound by traditional prejudices than in the case of [his opinion] of the Dissenters."[62] The Wesleys shared a significant amount of theological and liturgical common ground with Roman Catholics, which gave a hint of credibility to literary attacks like those of Bishop Lavington and to the misinformed and violent mobs who saw the Wesleys as crypo-Catholics who were just passing for Protestant Anglicans. The Wesleys spent the early decades of their ministry trying to distinguish and distance the Methodists from Roman Catholicism, hoping to avoid the rabid anti-Catholic sentiments that periodically swept through England like a tidal wave. The Methodists' own experiences of religious prejudice and persecution might have kindled compassion towards the persecuted Roman Catholics. John's *Open Letter to a Roman Catholic* (1749) and the Methodist mission to Ireland (beginning in 1747) showed they were capable of projecting a conciliatory and irenic tone towards Roman Catholics. But even while working diligently in Ireland, John did not really address "the Irish problem" that was rooted in centuries of British colonialism, extreme poverty, and the hopeless condition in which many Irish Roman Catholics lived. He also seemed unable to avoid the harmful stereotypes that situation generated.

The controversy surrounding the Catholic Relief Act of 1778 struck opposite chords with John and Charles Wesley. John gave voice to old fears about Roman Catholic disloyalty; fears had been well answered nearly a century before by John Gother's *A Papist Misrepresented* (1683)[63] and more recently by Richard Challoner (1691–1781), "the leading Papist of London."[64] John's alliance with the Protestant Association and the jingoistic Lord Gordon was both puzzling and reprehensible. Charles rightly viewed the Protestant Association as a group that merited his ridicule and criticism, but not his support.[65] John Wesley's "inconsistent sentiments of sincere toleration being mingled with blood-curdling talk of Popish cruelty and disloyalty"[66] left both religious tolerance and greater intolerance on the table as viable options for the next generation of Methodists. Regrettably, they chose the latter course, the path of intolerance and prejudice. "It is

61. C. Wesley and J. Wesley, *Poetical Works* VIII:267.
62. Rack, *Reasonable Enthusiast*, 309.
63. Gother, *Papist Misrepresented and Represented*, 37–41.
64. Butler, *Methodists and Papists*, 71.
65. C. Wesley and J. Wesley, *Poetical Works* VIII:449–87.
66. Rack, *Reasonable Enthusiast*, 309.

a sad fact," Henry Rack reported, "that early nineteenth century Wesley-ans became notorious for their anti-Catholic sentiments and opposition to Catholic emancipation, part of the blame must be attached to the tradition which Wesley had endorsed."[67]

QUESTIONS FOR FURTHER CONSIDERATION:

1. Jonathan Swift's statement about "just enough religion to hate" points out that religious sentiments can produce prejudice (instead of allevi-ating it). How does this happen? How can you avoid it?

2. What is the connection between religion, faith, fear, and religious prejudice? How can this be defused? Can this connection be used for redress instead of harm? How?

3. We have seen an example of how patriotism and religion can become interwoven in unwholesome ways. How can you discern when that is happening? What can you do to avoid it?

4. John's experiences in Ireland seemed to reinforce his negative stereo-types of Irish Catholics, whereas Charles's experience challenged the prejudices. How do you account for the difference? What can we learn from it?

5. Why does religious prejudice remain such a powerful force in today's world? What concerns, needs, or fears do you see it feeding on? What can you do to avoid or alleviate it?

67. Rack, *Reasonable Enthusiast*, 312.

CHAPTER 10

"The Pursuit of Happiness"

The Crisis Caused by Debilitating Popular Culture

THE PHRASE "THE PURSUIT of happiness" did not originate with the American Declaration of Independence. It belonged to the "the Age of Reason" and the thought-world which the framers of the Declaration shared with Georgian England.[1] As British philosopher John Locke (1632–1704) wrote in his *Essay Concerning Human Understanding* (1689): "The necessity of pursuing true happiness [is] the foundation of liberty."[2] Enlightenment thinkers on both sides of the Atlantic made reference to "their Creator" in their "pursuit of happiness"; it was always framed as a human right or liberty and as a worthy end in itself. Traditional Christianity thought of human happiness differently. When, for example, *The Westminster Shorter Catechism* (1647) asked: "What is the chief end of man?," the prescribed answer was: "To glorify God, and enjoy Him forever."[3] The shift that was underway in popular understanding of human happiness was subtle, but also significant. Where the Protestant statement pointed to God as both the cause and chief end of human happiness, the Enlightenment philosophers looked upon "the pursuit of happiness" as a human right and an end in itself. This intellectual shift could be called "the secularization of happiness" since it turned the focus from God to human culture and society.

The Georgian gentry, who sat at the pinnacle of the socioeconomic pyramid, were a leisure class. They had the free time, funds, mobility and

1. Hamilton, "Why Did Jefferson Change 'Property' to the 'Pursuit of Happiness?'"
2. Locke, *Essay Concerning Human Understanding* II:XXI.52.
3. Fisher, *Westminster Assembly's Shorter Catechism Explained*, 7.

social freedom (particularly if they were men) to pursue happiness on their own terms. The people below them on the "great chain of being" worked very hard to keep the gentry at the top. The work life of rural laborers followed a rhythm determined by the necessities caused by weather and the seasons. It was a pattern that did not have much leisure time built into it; religious holy days were the main exception. Domestic workers served at the whim of their masters and, like farm workers, they lacked the time, mobility, and funds to pursue happiness in a big way. This was true of most working people, with clergy and the other professions falling somewhere in between the opposite ends of the spectrum.

The gradual shift away from a predominately agrarian and agricultural society dramatically changed the work of many people. Leisure was no longer the sole possession of the landed gentry; rich industrialists, middle-class tradesmen, merchants, and even some skilled workers now had leisure time too.[4] With increased free time, funds, and mobility, and with a sociotheological backlash against the earlier restrictions of Puritan society, Georgian England experienced an exponential increase in the pursuit of happiness. The avenues of this pursuit varied greatly, as did the rationales, approaches, and intensity employed. Wealth and social class mattered a lot, and emerging middle-class people (particularly women) who were striving for respectability bore more restrictions than either the rich or the poor. The rich and the poor often pursued happiness with reckless abandon because the former had nothing to lose while the latter had nothing to gain. So relentless was the eighteenth-century pursuit of pleasure that commentators as diverse as poet Joseph Addison, painter William Hogarth, and novelists Henry Fielding, Daniel Defoe, and John Wesley all warned that the so-called "innocent diversions" pursed by many people had deleterious effects that were ruining the health and good character of the nation.

Joseph Addison (1672–1719) warned of the distraction of the mind and the diminishment of duty that occurs when people

> too frequently indulge ourselves in any of the most innocent diversions and entertainments, since the mind may insensibly fall off from the relish of virtuous actions, and by degrees, exchange that pleasure, which it takes in the performance of its duty, for delights of a much more inferior and unprofitable nature.[5]

Others, like the artist William Hogarth and practical theologian John Wesley, in their own way challenged the widely accepted notion that these so-called

4. Voth, "Time and Work in Eighteenth-Century London," 37.
5. Addison, *Spectator* III:447.

"innocent" or "harmless" diversions were actually innocent because of their harmful and exploitive effects. Wesley strongly warned against the danger of finding comfort in "all the idle diversions and amusements of the world, all the pleasures which 'perish in the using,' and which only tend to benumb and stupefy the soul, that it may be neither sensible of itself nor God."[6]

John Wesley often described these harmful innocent pastimes as "dissipation." He reported: "Almost in every part of our nation, more especially in the large and populous towns, we hear a general complaint among sensible persons of the still increasing 'dissipation.' It is observed to diffuse itself more and more in the court, the city, and the country."[7] On at least one occasion, in Wales, Charles Wesley attended "a revel at Lanvans to dissuade them from their *innocent* diversions in St. Peter's words, 'For the time past of our life may suffice us to have wrought the will of the gentiles, when we walked in lasciviousness, lusts, excess of wine, revellings, banqueting, and abominable idolatries' [1 Pet 4:3]." One woman "fell down under the stroke of the hammer" of Charles's evangelism, he reported, because she was so deeply convinced of the harmful potential of her "innocent pleasures, O that all her fellows might like-wise confess 'she that liveth in pleasures is dead while she liveth' [1 Tim 5:6]."[8]

The Georgian "Gin Craze" was one of the most obvious of these "dissipations," one which led to many others. Although the distillation of gin had begun in the previous century, its consumption became a social force and public health epidemic in the English eighteenth century. The local "gin mill" or café replaced the churches and community centers as the hub and mainstay of almost every neighborhood. "In 1721," Oscar Sherwin reported, "every tenth house sold liquor; in 1750 every fifth house in the city [of London] proper."[9] The gentry sipped gin at gentlemen's clubs, some of which were thinly disguised brothels, and at cafés, or at "sporting" events. Poor and hopeless people guzzled gin as a quick and cheap (though short-lived) escape from lives that were full of pain and hopelessness. As Lesley Solomonson explained: "While the rich drank for sport, the poor drank to forget their sordid existence, and drinking often led to grave misdeeds. Transcripts from England's Court of Record, the Old Bailey, frequently mention gin's damning influence."[10] A popular slogan seen posted on gin mills of the period read: "Drunk for a Penny, Dead Drunk for Two, Clean Straw for Free." It evidenced that the poor bought

6. J. Wesley, *Sermons* II:485.

7. J. Wesley, *Sermons* III:116.

8. C. Wesley, *Manuscript Journal* I:328. Emphasis original.

9. Sherwin, "Crime and Punishment," 170.

10. Solomonson, *Gin*, 49.

gin—not by the *drink*, but by the *drunk*. When they passed out from drinking, they were stacked up like human cord-wood on the "clean straw" to make room inside for more drinkers. "The slogan," reported historian Solomonson, "illustrates the enthusiasm of the masses toward consumption and the eagerness of suppliers to provide it."[11]

The novel-writing Chief Magistrate of London, Henry Fielding (1707–54), observed: "Gin is the principal sustenance of more than an hundred thousand people in this metropolis. Wretches swallow pints of this poison within twenty-four hours; the dreadful effects of which I have the misfortune every day to see, and to smell too."[12] In his professional life Fielding often witnessed the sway gin held over the populace and directly connected drunkenness with theft and robbery and worse: "I have plainly perceived from the state of the case, that the gin alone was the cause of the transgression, and have been sometimes sorry that I was obliged to commit them to prison."[13] Judge Fielding saw the health crisis caused by mass drunkenness among "the lower kind of people"; it ranged from a general loss "of the health and strength and the very being of numbers of his majesty's most useful subjects," to a tragic epidemic of the lifelong effects of prenatal alcohol syndrome.[14] "Should the drinking of this poison be continued in its present height during the next ten years," Fielding opined, "there will be few of the common people left to drink it."[15] Writing in 1736 in his *Distilled Spiritous Liquors: The Bane of the Nation*, Thomas Wilson observed: "The most valuable part of the nation was intoxicated by a fatal, slow but sure poison."[16]

Notice that the "lower kind of people" (Fielding), when seen from an economic point of view, were deemed "the most valuable part of the nation" (Wilson). When the social destruction and health burden of the epidemic of drunkenness was linked to the serious economic decline that resulted from it, a spate of Gin Acts flowed from Parliament over the course of thirty years. Beginning in 1721, these Gin Acts forced gin production to go "underground," where there was no regulation. The "bathtub gin" then produced was infamous for the harmful substances that were literally thrown in to mask the putrid flavor caused by avoiding costly ingredients, like juniper berries. The Gin Acts also stigmatized drunkenness as a scourge of low-class

11. Solomonson, *Gin*, 49.

12. Fielding, *Enquiry*, 28.

13. Fielding, *Enquiry*, 29.

14. Fielding, *Enquiry*, 30.

15. Fielding, *Enquiry*, 34.

16. Wilson, *Distilled Spirituous Liquors*, 2, 7, 29.

people, and contributed significantly to the isolation and alienation many workers felt, particularly working-class women.[17] The Gin Act of 1751, which required licensing and seriously restricted gin sales, put many of the neighborhood gin mills out of business and thereby curtailed gin consumption.

William Hogarth, *Gin Lane*, 1751, etching on paper, 38.9 x 32.2 cm, Metropolitan Museum of Modern Art, New York.

Artist William Hogarth (1687–1764) entered the gin debate through his side-by-side etchings of "Gin Lane" and "Beer Street" (1751). The more famous of the two, "Gin Lane," depicted the debauchery, chaos, and debilitating effects of the gin craze. Over against a background of riotous drunkenness, the picture's right foreground is dominated by an image of a drunken mother who has absentmindedly dropped her infant into the gutter. Hogarth's depiction of the drunken, unfit mother was probably inspired by the tragic case of alcoholic Judith Defour, who murdered her own child in 1734 in order to sell his new, donated clothes to buy gin.[18] Seated on a step just below the unfit mother in "Gin Street" is an emaciated man in a drunken stupor. His alcohol addiction is so acute he has neither the funds nor inclination for food, and his ribs and skull are clearly visible through his skin.

17. White, "'Slow But Sure Poyson,'" 37.
18. Dillon, *Gin*, 93–110.

In contrast to "Gin Lane," Hogarth's other print, "Beer Street," depicts a place of British congeniality where proper people enjoyed themselves over pints of wholesome English ale—the evil gin was invented in Denmark. Hogarth's artistic message was crystal clear: "Gin, bad; beer, good."[19] In the unlikely event the viewer missed his point, he also printed a poem along with the first edition of "Gin Lane":

William Hogarth, *Beer Street,* **1751, etching on paper, 39 x 32.5 cm, Metropolitan Museum of Modern Art, New York.**

Gin, cursed Fiend, with Fury fraught,
Makes human Race a Prey.
It enters by a deadly Draught
And steal our Life away.
Virtue and Truth, driv'n to Despair

19. William Hogarth, *Beer Street,* 1751, print, 39 x 32.5 cm, Metropolitan Museum of Modern Art, New York.

Its Rage compells to fly,
But cherishes with hellish Care
Theft, Murder, Perjury.
Damned Cup! that on the Vitals preys
That liquid Fire contains,
Which Madness to the heart conveys,
And rolls it thro' the Veins.

During his incessant ministerial travels, John Wesley saw plenty of drunkenness. His concern soon took shape in a small pamphlet, *A Word to a Drunkard* (1745), which he carried in his saddle bags for public distribution. He remembered one such occasion: "Many years ago," John reported, "passing a man in Moorfields, one who was so drunk he could not stand, I put a paper into his hand. He looked at it and said, "A Word to a Drunkard—that is me—Sir, Sir! I am wrong—I know I am wrong—Pray let me talk a little with you.' He held me by and a full half-hour," Wesley recalled, "And I believe [afterwards] he got drunk no more."[20] Wesley's message to drunkards began with compassion instead of blame, and he urged all those who would listen to take the same approach: "I beseech you, brethren, by the mercies of God, do not despise poor drunkards. Have compassion on them. Be instant with them in season and out of season!"[21] Wesley knew that problematic drinking often ran deeper than mere self-indulgence and bad choices; he recognized that many people had a life of pain and a hopeless heart that was being anesthetized with alcohol. So John Wesley told the Methodists to offer alcoholic persons words of comfort and support so that they did not "sink deeper [into despair] for [they think] none has any hope for them."[22]

John Wesley's *Word to a Drunkard* reminded drunken persons who they really were—not worthless drunks—but beloved children of God, created in God's own image. "God made you a man" he wrote, "but you make yourself a beast . . . You strip yourself of your understanding."[23] By abrogating their reason and understanding, the drunkard forfeited God's greatest gifts to humanity; which was really horrible Christian stewardship. Even worse, however, was/is the way excessive drinking stirs "up all the devilish tempers that are in you and others."[24] Wesley understood drunkenness as an indication of a deep, inner dilemma, more than a mere moral failing that

20. J. Wesley, *Sermons,* II:519.
21. J. Wesley, *Sermons,* II:519.
22. J. Wesley, *Sermons,* II:519.
23. J. Wesley, *Works* XI:169.
24. J. Wesley, *Works* XI:169.

required mere repentance. He urged drunken persons to look within themselves and resolve to become their best selves. And he urged them to pray to God to forgive and cleanse sin, to do a restorative work within them—a restorative work that they could not do for themselves. They were to pray to become sensible to the love and acceptance of God, so that the former drunkard could say: "I may go and sin no more, that I may love much having had so much forgiven!"[25] While his published tract did not explicitly say so, it is implicit that the community, accountability, and practical support of the Methodist infrastructure were an important part of Wesley's prescription for the alcoholic person's recovery and health. The support of the Methodist Society, when wedded to Wesley's *Word to a Drunkard*, foreshadowed the "Twelve Step" programs that continue to help people battle addictions.[26] And, as we noted elsewhere, John Wesley's *On the Present Scarcity of Provisions* linked rampant distillation of grain with the results of poverty, hunger, and destitution. This too is very poor stewardship; a better and less harmful way to waste such a valuable resource, Wesley mused, would be "throwing it into the sea," instead of "converting it into deadly poison; poison that naturally destroys not only the strength and life, but also the morals, of our countrymen."[27]

Lawrence Stone observed: "Freedom of sexual expression was one of many by-products of the eighteenth century pursuit of happiness."[28] Roy Porter saw this "freedom" beginning with a leisured class reaction to the Puritan values that dominated the previous century: "Amongst the affluent and leisured, sexuality thawed out," he wrote, "the libido was liberated."[29] Karen Harvey simply dubbed the English eighteenth century as "The Century of Sex."[30] This sexual "thaw" did not occur in a vacuum, and what is said about the bawdy character of eighteenth-century life must be set in the larger context brought about by the economic and social influences like class privilege, patriarchy, the permissiveness of the Age of Reason, and the gin epidemic.

The bawdy character of the Georgian age signaled a widespread discovery of "the joy of sex." Sex was no longer seen only as a "marital duty," one to be reserved for procreation (as the Puritans insisted). It became a significant part of the culturewide pursuit of happiness. Hence, Thomas

25. J. Wesley, *Works* XI:171.

26. Miskelly, "Restoration," completed in partial fulfillment of the requirements of Doctor of Ministry in the Divinity School of Duke University, 2016, illustrates this point very well.

27. J. Wesley, *Works* XI:54–55.

28. Stone, *Family, Sex and Marriage*, 328.

29. Porter, *English Society*, 278.

30. Harvey, "Century of Sex," 899–900.

Laqueur wrote: "Sometime in the eighteenth century, sex as we know it was invented."[31] The increased sexual freedom enjoyed by some, particularly young men of the gentry, exacerbated the double standard that had long existed between men and women, along with the many privileges of the upper class. Stone reported:

> The idea of the double standard persisted and continued to be translated into practice in real life. Young men of the upper classes were expected to have had some or even a good deal of pre-marital sexual experiences with prostitutes, serving-maids, courtesans, or foreign married women on the Grand Tour. Young women of the same class, however, nearly all carefully preserved their virginity, since its loss seriously damaged their value in the marriage market.[32]

Recent research indicates that by the 1770s, roughly 20 percent of the population of London over the age of 35 suffered from syphilis. Factors like the gin craze and the loosened sexual inhibitions of the so-called "century of sex" contributed to this epidemic, but researchers Szeter and Siena also point out that the precarious economic and working conditions of many young women played a significant role as well.[33]

Aristocratic marriages were still often carefully arranged, like a corporate merger. Aristocratic women were expected to remain virginal, to "do their marital duty," in order to find material security in their marriage, and—perhaps—pursue their happiness elsewhere. Middle-class women seemed to have less sexual freedom before and in marriage because they associated respectability with social advancement; while poor women often did whatever they needed to do to survive. "Place's Law" that "poverty and chastity are incompatible" rang true for far too many women in eighteenth-century England.[34] The anonymity that came with the growing populations of urban life also brought with it more sexual freedom than did life in a small, rural village.

31. Laqueur, *Making Sex*, 149.
32. Stone, *Family, Sex, and Marriage*, 544.
33. Szreter and Sierna, "Pox in Boswell's London."
34. Stone, *Family, Sex, and Marriage*, 616–18.

William Hogarth, *A Rake's Progress, Plate 3*, 1735, "The Orgy" etching on paper, 35.4 x 40.5, Metropolitan Museum of Modern Art, New York.

William Hogarth, *A Rake's Progress, Plate 8*, 1735, "The Madhouse," etching on paper, 35.4 x 40.5, Metropolitan Museum of Modern Art, New York.

The "rake," or playboy of the Georgian era, was, as Jude Knight described him, "lewd, debauched, and womanizing. Rakes gambled, partied, and drank hard and they pursued their pleasures with cold calculation. Then as now, rakes were self-centered narcissists who acknowledged no moral code, and no external restraint either."[35] The "rake" was sometimes romanticized in British literature, as in Henry Fielding's *Tom Jones,* but in real life he was much less appealing. As William Hogarth chronicled "A Rake's Progress" (1735), through eight paintings, he made it clear that there was a high price to be paid for a playboy lifestyle. Hogarth's anti-hero, Tom Rakewell, began his all-out pursuit of happiness with the rejection of his pregnant fiancé so that he could receive a larger dowry by marrying another woman. His pursuit of pleasure led him step by step to a gentlemen's club ("The Levee"), to "The Orgy" (above), and "The Gaming House," only to land him, less happily, in Debtor's Prison (plate 7), and finally, "The Madhouse," where—wracked by disease—Rakewell lost his sanity and then lost his life. Novelist Daniel Defoe also warned against "the *Conjugal Lewdness* or wide-spread fornication and adultery" he saw in the emerging café culture of Georgian England.[36] Moralists like Hogarth and Defoe offered a perspective on pleasure with which the early Methodists agreed.

The Wesley brothers advocated and (so far as we know) practiced sexual abstinence prior to marriage, and fidelity within marriage, which they also enjoined upon the Methodists. They considered "adultery, and fornication to be works of the flesh" and emblems of a pre-Christian life; one that is not guided by the fruit of the Spirit (Gal 5:19).[37] "The lust of the flesh"—that is, "gluttony, or drunkenness, luxury or sensuality, fornication"—was set in contradistinction to a life guided by God the Holy Spirit, because it resulted in "uncleanness, defiling that body which was designed to be a temple of the Holy Ghost" (cf. 1 Cor 6:19).[38] Even the "Almost Christian," in John Wesley's view, "avoids all actual adultery, fornication, and uncleanness, but [also] every work or look, that either directly or indirectly tends thereto."[39] But being a Methodist Christian was not defined by these or other prohibitions, rather by having that faith in Christ "which 'purifies the heart,' by the power of God who dwelleth therein, from pride, anger, desire, 'from all unrighteousness' [1 John 1:9]."[40]

35. Knight, "Rakehell in Fact and Fiction," para. 4.
36. Defoe, *Conjugal Lewdness, or Matrimonial Whoredom,* 64–69.
37. J. Wesley, *Sermons* I:236.
38. J. Wesley, *Sermons* I:227.
39. J. Wesley, *Sermons* I:132–33.
40. J. Wesley, *Sermons* I:133.

Living in "the century of sex," John Wesley looked around himself and drew parallels to the antediluvian immorality that caused God to destroy the world by flood.[41] Against this backdrop, he pointed to the transformed lives of those who *had been* "whoremongers" as evidence of the great work God was doing in England through the Methodists.[42] And when he replied to "N.D.'s" query, published in the *Bath Journal*, "Why I do not warn the members of our Society against fornication and adultery?," John explained: "I answer, for the same reason that I do not warn them against . . . murder. Namely, because I do not apprehend them to be in immediate danger thereof . . ."[43] But the Methodists *were* in "immediate danger," as were the Wesley brothers themselves, because—as Henry Abelove pointed out in *The Evangelist of Desire*—the emotional connection between *agape* (the love of God) and *eros* (human physical love) is more powerful than they admitted. Damaging gossip and popular critiques certainly anticipated that connection and pointed to the Wesley brothers' bigamist brother-in-law, Wesley Hall, or philandering Methodist preachers like James Wheatley, and oddly named Methodist practices like "the Love Feast," as evidences of it.[44] When John too readily believed Wheatley's false denials of immorality, the contagion soon spread to other preachers as well.[45]

John Wesley's unusual familiarity with women, three bungled courtships, and a disastrous marriage to Mary Vazeille Wesley made him the frequent target of gossip and false (so far as we know) charges of immorality. As Alan Rose reported, "Wesley himself was pursued by scandal, to some extent even in the private gossip and correspondence of his followers. His fondness for warm though pastoral correspondence with young women was lamented and criticized as indiscreet and embarrassing even though basically innocent if naïve."[46] John's angry wife, Mary, fueled the fires of gossip by charging him with "running after strange women," most notably Sarah Ryan, and by then circulating damaging excerpts from her husband's correspondence.[47] Prior to his marriage, in 1744, Elizabeth Story reported Charles Wesley to Bishop Gibson for "committing or offering to commit lewdness with her." Charles's unequivocal denial to the bishop, supported by corroborating testimony from others, caused Story to drop the charge,

41. J. Wesley, *Sermons* II:558; III:223.

42. J. Wesley, *Works* VIII:402.

43. J. Wesley, *Letters* II:358.

44. Lyles, *Methodism Mocked*, 68–71, 89–91.

45. Leger, *John Wesley's Last Love*, 115–18.

46. Rack, "But Lord, Let It Be Betsy," 3.

47. Lloyd, "'Running after Strange Women,'" 173.

which she ultimately confessed she made out of vengeance.[48] But at least one of his colleagues, Charles reported, "desired my answer to the many horrid scandals Thomas Williams has raised against me, e.g., my keeping 20 mistresses only in London, etc. I simply denied them all, which was all the satisfaction I could give him."[49] Charles's loving marriage and reciprocal relationship with his wife, Sarah "Sally" Gwynne Wesley, while not without its challenges, silenced much of the gossip about him and was a happy counterpoint to his brother John's.[50]

Based on what can be ascertained from journals, popular literature, and the theatre, homosexuality was fairly common in Georgian England, but since it was stigmatized by popular culture and punished by law, gay life was also often quite clandestine. Persecution gradually diminished due to more relaxed sexual attitudes. Scholars of the early modern period, for example, point to "a sodomy paranoia paralleling the witch burning craze." By 1749, public executions for "sodomy" averaged about one per year.[51] But a queer person still lived a closeted lifestyle, often caught in conflict between their same-sex desires and the deep disapproval of their family, friends, society, and church.[52] By 1700, a so-called sodomite subculture flourished in London, that "could claim defined meeting places—parks, latrines, public arcades and certain taverns."[53] "Molly Houses," like the one Vere Street, London, were safe places for male homosexuals to socialize, meet for casual sex, or to find long-term partners.[54] John and Charles Wesley reported no direct contact with or ministry to gay people (so far as they knew). They followed the traditional reading of the Scriptures which associated homosexuality with sin (this will be explored more fully in chapter 18). In John's treatise *The Doctrine of Original Sin* (1758), for example, "the Sodomites and Antediluvians" were examples of the sway sin holds over fallen humanity.[55]

In the last third of the Georgia era, a foppish and effeminate male figure emerged as the alter ego of the playboy rake. Where the rake's masculinity was exhibited and verified through his sexual exploitation of women, the so-called "macaronis" were gender-bending young men whose sexuality was ambiguous. These young gentlemen returned from their "Grand Tour" of

48. See Maddox and Underhill, "Untangling the Tangled Web."
49. C. Wesley, *Manuscript Journal* II:423.
50. Tyson, *Assist Me to Proclaim*, 153–71.
51. Gerard and Heckma, *Pursuit of Sodomy*, 110–13.
52. Gleckner, *Gray Agonistes*, 13–14.
53. Byrne, *Road to Stonewall*, 7.
54. Byrne, *Road to Stonewall*, 10. Cf. Norton, "Raid on Mother Clap's Molly House."
55. J. Wesley, *Works* IX:251; 445.

Europe with a particular taste for Italian culture, fashion, and food—which they borrowed and by exaggeration made into a style of their own. They were described and soundly lampooned by *The Oxford Magazine* (1770):

> There is indeed a kind of animal, neither male nor female, a thing of the neuter gender, lately started among us. It is called a macaroni. It talks without meaning, it smiles without pleasantry, it eats without appetite, it rides without exercise, it wenches without passion.[56]

Rictor Norton explained, "Theatrical mannerisms and clothing that was fashionable to the point of burlesque were characteristics of the macaroni, whose signature was an elaborate wig, often with an enormous pigtail."[57]

Samuel Hieronymous Green, *What Is This My Son Tom?*, **1774, print on paper, Library of Congress, cp. 3c 15003.**

56. Shipley, *Origins of English Words*, 143.
57. Norton, "Macaroni Club," 4.

"In so far as the Macaronies aped ladies' fashions," Norton reported, "they were deemed to be effeminate and sexually indeterminate."[58] In 1764, Horace Walpole's correspondence alluded to the formation of the Macaroni Club in London which within a decade had become the focal point for several prominent "homosexual scandals."[59] And, as Peter McNeil explained, "as soon as the macaroni stereotype entered the middle class press the character was interpreted as sodomitical."[60] Historical context adds new sting to the old song "Yankee Doodle" which the British troops used to ridicule George Washington and the American rebels a decade later: "Yankee Doodle went to town/A-riding on a pony,/Stuck a feather in his cap,/And called it macaroni."[61] "Doodle" was a derisive term for a country bumpkin, who in this ballad tried to copy the newest urban style and only wound up looking foolish—if not also queer.

Charles Wesley's personal tastes were significantly less puritanical than his spartan brother John's. But Charles had no time or respect for the way the gentrified leisure class wasted their lives on superficial manners, foppish styles, and dissipating pastimes. Charles may have had the macaronis in mind when he penned (in the mid-1770s) this hymnological critique of "a modern man of fashion"[62]:

> What is a modern man of fashion?
> A man of taste and dissipation;
> A busy man, without employment;
> A happy man without enjoyment;
> Who squanders all his time and treasures
> In empty joys, and tasteless pleasures;
> Visits, attendance, and attention,
> And courtly arts too low to mention,
> In sleep, and dress, and sport and play,
> He throws his worthless life away;
> Has no opinions of his own,
> But takes from leading beaux the *ton*;
> Born to be flatter'd and to flatter,
> The most important *thing* in nature,
> Wrapp'd up in self-sufficient pride,
> With his own virtues satisfied,

58. Norton, "Macaroni Club," 4.

59. Norton, "Macaroni Club," 1.

60. Segal, "That Diss Song Known as 'Yankee Doodle,'" paras. 8–9. Cf. McNeil, *Pretty Gentlemen*.

61. Waters, "Macaroni in 'Yankee Doodle' Is Not What You Think."

62. C. Wesley, *Representative Verse*, 330.

With a disdainful smile or frown
He on the riffraff crowd looks down;
The world polite, his friends and he,
All the rest are—no body.

Taught by the great his smiles to sell,
And how to write and how to spell,
The great his oracles he makes,
Copies their vices and mistakes,
Custom pursues, his only rule,
And lives an ape, and dies a fool![63]

While many people saw increased sexual expression as a "harmless diversion" or "victimless crime," it often led to the victimization and oppression of women and men. This was most often true for women in domestic service, indentured or otherwise, and women who lived in poverty or on the edge of it. Women who pushed themselves forward into male-dominated fields, like careers in music or the theatre, were often assumed to be supplementing their income or advancement with prostitution. The life of a sex worker was extremely precarious; violence against these women was very common, almost never reported, and rarely prosecuted. Sadly, Jessica Steinberg's assessment of the eighteenth-century situation could have been written just yesterday:

> Given that most prostitutes were poor women who lacked the necessary resources to prosecute the offenders, we can assume that a considerable amount of the violence that prostitutes endured went unreported. But even for those who were interested in prosecuting their assailant, their reputation as a prostitute would have all but assured the case to have been dismissed or settled against them.[64]

When the London newspapers reported the murder of streetwalkers, they reflected common public sentiments: "These prostitutes were portrayed as being at least partly the blame for their demise."[65]

When William Hogarth examined "A Harlot's Progress" through a series of six paintings and etchings (1732), he explored the flip side of "The Rake's Progress," by shifting his focus from predator to prey.[66] Hogarth's heroine, Moll Hackabout, was depicted more as a victim of cruel events

---

63. C. Wesley and J. Wesley, *Poetical Works* VIII:478–80.

64. Steinberg, *Seven Deadly Sins of Prostitution*, 247.

65. Steinberg, *Seven Deadly Sins of Prostitution*, 250.

66. See above, p. 74.

than a perpetrator of wrongdoing. The only other mourners at Moll's wake were a former "John," three of her co-workers, and her orphaned, young son. Hogarth's art chronicled the tragic side of the prostitute's story. Moll was depicted as a victim of social and economic forces that were beyond her control. Those who viewed Moll's plight were more likely inspired to mourn, and perhaps agitate for change, than to condemn her. This sentiment was echoed in many of the "Whore Novels" published in the first half of the English eighteenth century, some of which, like Daniel Defoe's *Moll Flanders* (1722) and *Roxane: The Fortunate Mistress* (1724), were fictional character studies loaded with significant social import. John Wesley's pastoral ministry to the streetwalkers he met in his itineracy was explored above (in chapter 7); here it is worth recalling, however, that he viewed them, borrowing the title of his treatise, as "an unhappy woman."[67] In his mind, people trapped in the sex trade were more apt to be victims than rank sinners or "common whores." His approach with them was one of acceptance, repentance, and restoration, as he hoped that the Methodists by God's grace could help the "unhappy woman" reclaim her truest self as a child of God.

Henry Alken, *The Bull Baiting*, c. 1894, oil on paper, 17.8 x 26 cm.

The amusements of an age function as windows into society's soul. The great popularity of "blood sports" like bull baiting, cock fighting, dog fighting, bear-baiting, duck-baiting, goose-pulling, and fox hunting, in which various kinds of animals were horribly maimed or killed for the enjoyment

67. See "A Word to an Unhappy Woman," in J. Wesley, *Works* XI:171–73.

of paying customers and gamblers, seems almost inexplicable to modern readers. But perhaps not, considering the current popularity of "ultimate fighting" and fighting dogs. In England, blood sports had been popular for centuries, but they had a great resurgence in the Georgian era. Beyond the horrible fascination of the macabre, the popularity of blood sports should be seen as a part of the same testing of older social mores and values that went along with "the gin craze" and the "joy of sex." There was also some class-crashing going on as gents and middle-class people indulged in spectacles that had originated with the predominately poor, lower-class, rural culture.[68] John Wesley described blood sports as the "foul remains of Gothic barbarity" and "a reproach not only to all religion, but even to human nature."[69] He saw many examples of events during his travels, and on several occasions they directly impeded his ministry.[70] Market days, even in Smithfield or Whitechapel in London, were punctuated with "bullock hunting."

On at least one occasion, a bull-baiting event was staged in the middle of John's outdoor preaching service at Pensford, where "a great company of rabble . . . came furiously upon us, bringing a bull which they had been baiting, and now drove him in among the people."[71] No one was injured, excepting the bull, but twice Wesley had to take its snout in his hands and push it away from himself to keep the bull's blood from covering his clothing.[72] So pervasive was the cruelty of the age that William Hogarth felt compelled to illustrate its growth and development through a pictorial study of the life of the fictional young boy, Tom Nero, as he moved through "The Four Stages of Cruelty" (1751). Tom's tormenting of a dog, which passersby ignored, evidenced cultural fascination for cruelty that blossomed into blood sports ("First Stage of Cruelty," plate 1), violence in the streets, and a ghoulish interest in dismemberment and medical experimentation (plate 4). Towards the end of his ministry, however, John Wesley believed that England's fascination with blood sports was waning: "Bear-baiting also is now very seldom seen, and bull-baiting not very often," he wrote. "And it seems cock-fighting would totally cease in England, were it not for two or three right honorable patrons."[73] Rightly so or not, John Wesley believed Methodism's growth contributed to the decline of blood sports.

---

68. Parratt, "Robert W. Malcolmson's 'Popular Recreations,'" 312–23.

69. J. Wesley, *Sermons* III:272.

70. J. Wesley, *Journal and Diaries* II:169, 218, 319; V:74; VII:38.

71. J. Wesley, *Journal and Diaries* II:257.

72. J. Wesley, *Journal and Diaries* II:257.

73. See "More Excellent Way," in J. Wesley, *Sermons* III:272.

William Hogarth, *The First Stage of Cruelty,* **1751, print, 40.5 x 33.5 cm,
Metropolitan Museum of Modern Art, New York.**

Cardplaying was another craze that swept Georgian England; more than two dozen different games were mentioned in the contemporary literature.[74] "By the time George II came to the throne in 1727," wrote historian Felicity Day, "Britain was a nation addicted to gambling." Like many modern casinos, London's many gambling houses never closed. Much of the attraction of blood sports was found in the side bets and wagers that went on between spectators.[75] Gambling at cards or dice was also the staple entertainment at house parties, assembly rooms, gentlemen's clubs, and spa resorts. Gambling at cards figures prominently in contemporary literature, like Alexander Pope's *Rape of the Lock* (1712) and Daniel Defoe's *Roxane* (1724), for example, and in each case it leads to debilitating results. Popular card games like Hazard and Faro brought with them such catastrophic gambling losses that, in 1710, the government issued a Gambling Act, prohibiting any gambling debt above £10; subsequent Gambling Acts tried to make several particularly addictive card games illegal, but these proved to be unenforceable. While well intentioned, the Gambling Acts generally had the opposite effect of what was planned because forbidden gambling was

74. Hudson, "Pastimes in the Georgian Era."
75. Day, "Nation Addicted to Gaming," paras. 1–2.

even more thrilling than legal gambling. Probation both increased gambling and drove it underground to be carried out in unregulated and clandestine locations.[76]

Since the dangers of gambling seemed less obvious than some, John Wesley attacked it with surprising clarity and frequency.[77] Opposition to gambling was implied in the Methodist "General Rules," since it is generally acknowledged that gambling falls under the list of "such diversions as cannot be used in the name of Lord Jesus."[78] In Wesley's view, gambling was/ is quintessential poor stewardship. Its addictive power robs both God and the poor of their due. Despite this, some people argued they gambled a little for pleasure and without harm. To these people, Wesley urged: "Consider your neighbor . . . we cannot devour the increase of his lands, or perhaps the lands and houses themselves by gaming, by overgrown bills . . . or by requiring or taking such interest as even the laws of our country forbid."[79]

John Wesley critiqued these "harmless diversions" from a theological perspective. He believed that the pursuit of happiness must be seen from a God-centered point of view. This was the fundamental flaw he saw in the way too many people went about popular pastimes. They pursued happiness as an end in itself, rather than a means to the greater end of enjoying God through God's good creations. John's fondness for a saying from the philosopher Blaise Pascal (1623–62) described his priorities very well: "While the generality of men use God and enjoy the world, we on the contrary only use the world while we enjoy God."[80] Those particular things which had the power to turn a person's heart and life away from God, and evoke in them "the love of the world," John Wesley described as "dissipations." He recognized that most people "confine this character to those who are violently attached to women, gaming, drinking; to dancing, balls, races, or the poor, childish diversion of running foxes and hares out of breath." But that is to miss the fundamental point: "It equally belongs to the serious fool who forgets God by a close attention to *any* worldly employment."[81] Misplaced priorities of any sort, including vocational passion or undue professional involvement, lead to dissipation.

---

76. Day, "Nation Addicted to Gambling," 3–4.

77. See J. Wesley, *Sermons* II:52, 54, and 150, for example.

78. For the Methodist "General Rules," visit the website: https://www.umc.org/en/content/the-general-rules-of-the-methodist-church.

79. J. Wesley, *Sermons* II:270–71.

80. J. Wesley, *Letters* I:270.

81. J. Wesley, *Sermons* III:120 Emphasis added.

The God-focused life, for the Wesleyan Christian, was to be lived as a life of stewardship. The call to be "a good steward," or "a faithful and wise steward" of one's life, was sounded throughout John Wesley's published sermons.[82] His basic definition of stewardship focused upon the attitude with which one embraces life; we are indebted to God for all we are and all we have, and this realization should impel a person through life with deep gratitude, as well as with the desire to be faithful to God and productive for the greater good. The Christian steward does not own themself or the talents and material gifts bestowed upon them by God; these all belong to God and are given for our good and grateful service to God and to others. This meant "that there is no employment of our time, no action or conversation, that is purely indifferent. All is good or bad, because all our time, as everything we have, is not our own. All these are . . . the property of another—of God, our Creator."[83] This point of view clearly undercut the Georgian notion that some diversions were harmless or innocent, assuming they were morally innocuous contributions to the pursuit of happiness.

Despite the frenetic way John Wesley lived his own life, he did not want the Methodists "always intent upon business; both our bodies and minds require some relaxation. We need intervals of diversion from business. It will be necessary to be very explicit upon this head, as it is a point which has been much misunderstood."[84] Wesley believed that many pursuits of happiness, which sometime passed for "harmless diversions," "are a reproach, not only to all religion, but even to human nature."[85] Other diversions, while being not notoriously evil, endanger a person's conscience because they *have a tendency* towards "profaneness and debauchery."[86] Both Wesleys embraced fresh air and exercise as laudable diversions: long walks and gardening were common examples they offered. They favored listening to music, but John was particularly ambivalent about attending the balls, masquerades, or the theater: "I could not do it with a clear conscience; at least not in an English theater, the sink of all profaneness and debauchery;

---

82. See "The Great Assize," in J. Wesley, *Sermons*, I:354–75; "Sermon on the Mount, #8," in J. Wesley, *Sermons* I:612–32; "On Satan's Devices," in J. Wesley, *Sermons*, II:125–38; "The Use of Money," in J. Wesley, *Sermons*, II:263–81; "The Good Steward," in J. Wesley, *Sermons*, II:281–300; "The Danger of Riches," in J. Wesley, *Sermons*, III:227–47; "On Dress," in J. Wesley, *Sermons*, III:247–62; and "The Danger of Riches," in J. Wesley, *Sermons*, IV:177–87, for example.

83. J. Wesley, *Sermons* II:297.

84. J. Wesley, *Sermons* III:272.

85. J. Wesley, *Sermons* III:272.

86. J. Wesley, *Sermons* III:272.

but possibly others can."[87] Cardplaying and social dancing he also viewed as harboring the potential of "profaneness and debauchery."[88] Reading and cultivating one's mind he heartily affirmed, and showed a marked preference for religious literature, natural history, and current events.[89] In short, John Wesley thought whatever a Methodist did for recreation should be able to be done as a form of prayer—giving glory to God.[90]

Their selective approach to popular diversions meant that the Methodists needed to create an alternative to the lifestyle that was different from the way many of their contemporaries' pursued happiness. Their leisure had a spiritual dimension to it, and this concern gave birth to creative alternatives. Drunken nights at the tavern or gin mill were to be replaced by Christian fellowship and service; the Wesleyan Watch Night service was offered instead of Saturday nights of pubbing. Charles Wesley's hymns, which were amenable to all the popular tunes, were offered as replacements for bawdy and profane music. John Wesley's thirty-volume *Christian Library* provided reading material that served the same purpose, as did his *Arminian Magazine*. John even tried to redeem the somewhat questionable (in his mind) practice of cardplaying by creating Scripture playing cards as he tried unsuccessfully to turn it into a teaching moment for biblical truths.

QUESTIONS FOR FURTHER CONSIDERATION:

1. Is your theology of stewardship broad enough to inform the choices you make about your body, time, talents, and funds?

2. Do your recognize that many diversions—while seemingly innocent in themselves—can be detrimental because they have the capacity to harm others or divert us from better things?

3. Do you see leisure time and avocations as a spiritual matter? Why, or why not?

4. Does your own critique of harmful behaviors like drunkenness, exploitive sex, and gambling avoid casting blame upon those who are victims of them? Does it help them?

5. Does your critique of various harmful or wasteful diversions also include constructive alternatives to them?

87. J. Wesley, *Sermons* III:273.
88. J. Wesley, *Sermons* III:273.
89. J. Wesley, *Sermons* III:273.
90. J. Wesley, *Sermons* III:274.

Conclusion

WE HAVE COME TO the end of the first half of the narration of the Methodist family story. Along the way you have met a few of the women and men, spiritual relatives and friends, who have contributed so very much to who we are. The Methodists have journeyed long and far from London 1738. We have been preceded by "a great cloud of witnesses" (Heb 12:1–2) who have been our shapers and are our exemplars. They have left us concrete examples of what it looks like to try to live out Mr. Wesley's mandate: "to spread Scriptural holiness across the land, beginning with the Church."[1] Because of their deep love for the Church and not in spite of it, the early Methodists tried to breathe new life into it, but as they tried to pour new wine into old wine skins, they sometimes strained the seams of fellowship and ecclesial unity to the breaking point. For all their ardor for the church, they also thought they saw all too well the church's failures which emerged either by the church not doing some things well, and sometimes by doing nothing at all. Our forerunners took on many of the challenges that faced their church and their nation with great compassion, courage, and incredible spiritual energy. Subsequently, and perhaps by accident, the Methodist movement became *a* church, and then many church*es*, and as they did so, they alleviated some of the institutional problems that plagued their predecessors, but they also created new ones. Yet, they continued to love God and they gave themselves to helping the hopeless, poor, sick, hungry, excluded, oppressed, and marginalized people who were their neighbors. They were people following Christ in the Methodist mode, and they set a high standard to which we may aspire and from which we might learn; a pattern which we can hope and pray to be able to replicate.

It is comforting to remember that "the people called Methodists" have always cared deeply about being witnesses to God's love and acceptance in all facets of human life. This passion shaped the "all" aspect of the Methodist

1. J. Wesley, *Works*, VIII:299.

message: "*all* people can be saved; *all* people can know they are saved; *all* people can be saved to the uttermost." It was their creed, as well as their mission statement. It told them *where* to preach, *what* to preach, and *to whom* they must minister; it showed them *where* and *with whom* they must take a stand. It sharpened their perception of class privilege, economic disparity, and hurtful prejudices of any sort, and it fueled their concern about the self-centered and irresponsible use of finite recourses (like the barley wasted in the manufacture of gin) and occasionally caused them to challenge the economics of British colonialism, with its chattel slavery and wars of conquest. It caused them to question the debilitating pursuit of happiness through their society's "harmless diversions"—which were actually very harmful and exploitive for many people, particularly for poor and working-class people. Their profound optimism, rooted in the gospel of God's grace that gave the Methodists both the hope that they could make a difference in the world, as well as the tenacity to try, allowed them to affirm and seek the full potential that God placed in all of God's children, even when others said there was none. Whether it was classism, chauvinism, religious bigotry, racism, slavery, or wage slavery, they saw and often opposed oppression and exploitation—not only in their own lives, but in the lives of others as well.

The Methodist preoccupation with "methods" or rules can be traced to Susanna Wesley's little school in the Epworth manse, and to the Wesleyan penchant for good order which manifested itself in John Wesley's concern that the Methodists would not become "a rope of sand" with no connection to each other's lives. The "three simple rules," enshrined in the *Large Minutes,* encapsulate the Methodist method: "do no harm [to people's bodies and souls]," "do all the good you can [also to people's bodies and souls]," and attend to the five life-giving "means of grace [i.e., prayer, Scripture study, acts of self-denial, frequent communion, and the *koinonia* of close Christian fellowship]."[2] These rules evidence the Methodist's belief that spiritual *homeostasis* can best be found through living out the life of faith in ways punctuated by works of piety and works of mercy.

The volume that follows, *Shaped by Controversy,* accompanies the Methodists through the growing pains and controversies that occurred as the Methodist movement became *the* Methodist Church, and then very soon the Methodist church*es.* In this process, the Methodists went through significant internal strife and family trauma that forever shaped them—for good and for ill. These challenges were exemplified in eight major theological, ecclesial, and ethical controversies. These tried the values, tested the

---

2. See Job, *Three Simple Rules.* See also the small-group study guide, Finley, *Three Simple Rules for Christian Living.*

patience, strained familial relationships, and ultimately divided the Methodist movement. Among these were and have been: (1) the nature of spiritual life, faith, and good works; (2) controversy over predestination and the comforts of Christian salvation; (3) the difficulties of living out Christian Perfection in real life, among imperfect people; (4) the pain and trauma of ecclesiastical separation; (5) controversy over women's leadership; (6) the debilitating effects of racism and racial segregation; (7) controversy over institutional governance and shared leadership; and most recently (8) conflict over the affirmation and full inclusion of LGBTQI people. These interfamily squabbles have challenged, changed, and deeply pained the Methodists. But they have also forced them to examine their priorities and clarify what matters most to them. In each case, however, there are lessons to be learned about the ongoing challenges of vital piety, wealth, power, acceptance, prejudice, and the temptations of respectability, of institutional growth, or of survival. Each of these historic controversies is examined in the second volume of this study, *Shaped by Controversy*.

Bibliography

Abbott, Susannah. "Clerical Responses to the Jacobite Rebellion in 1715." *Historical Research* 76.193 (August 2003) 332–46.

Addison, Joseph. *The Spectator: A New Edition.* 8 vols. London: Routledge, 1891.

Allestree, Richard. *The Whole Duty of Man Laid Down in a Plain and Familiar Way For the Use of All, But Especially the Meanest Reader, With Private Devotions For Several Occasions.* London: SPCK, 1658.

Andrews, Dee. *Methodists in Revolutionary America.* Princeton: Princeton University Press, 2000.

Asbury, Francis. *The Journal and Letters of Francis Asbury.* 3 vols. Edited by Elmer Clark. Nashville: Abingdon, 1958.

Berger, Teresa. "Charles Wesley and Roman Catholicism." In *Charles Wesley: Poet and Theologian*, edited by S. T. Kimbrough, 205–21. Nashville: Abingdon/Kingswood, 1992.

Black, John Bennett. *The Reign of Queen Elizabeth.* Oxford: Clarendon, 1959.

Blain, Keisha N. "Enslaved People in Eighteenth-Century Britain." *Black Perspectives*, October 10, 2018. https://www.aaihs.org/enslaved-people-in-eighteenth-century-britain-an-interview-with-nelson-mundell/.

Blane, Rodney M. "Notes and Documents: Philip Thicknesse's Reminiscences of Early Georgia." *Georgia Historical Quarterly* 74 (Winter 1990) 672–98.

The Book of Homilies: A Critical Edition. Edited by Gerald Bray. London: Clarke and Co., 2015.

Boswell, James. *The Life of Samuel Johnson: Complete and Unabridged.* New York: Modern Library, 1936.

Brendlinger, Irv. *Social Justice Through the Eyes of Wesley: John Wesley's Theological Challenge to Slavery.* Kitchener, ON: Joshua, 2006.

———. "Wesley, Whitefield, a Philadelphia Quaker, and Slavery." *Wesleyan Theological Journal* 36.2 (Fall 2001) 164–74.

Brine, M. E. "Burial in Woollen." *Devon Heritage,* July 31, 2009. http://www.devonheritage.org/Nonplace/Genealogy/BurialinWoollen.htm.

"The British Beehive: How Victorian Society Saw Itself." *Cruikshankart.* https://www.cruikshankart.com/articles/british-beehive.html.

Butler, David. *Methodists and Papists: John Wesley and the Catholic Church in the Eighteenth Century.* London: Darton, Longman & Todd, 1995.

Byrne, Fone. *A Road to Stonewall: Male Homosexuality and Homophodia in English and American Literature, 1750–1969.* New York: Twayne, 1995.

Byrom, John. *The Private Journal and Literary Remains of John Byrom*. Edited by Richard Parker. 2 vols. Manchester: Chetham Society, 1888.

Campbell, Ted. *John Wesley and Christian Antiquity*. Nashville: Kingswood, 1991.

Canny, Nicholas P. "The Ideology of English Colonization: From Ireland to America." *William and Mary Quarterly* 30 (October 1973) 575–98.

Charleston, Libby-Jane. "The Truth Behind Queen Elizabeth's White 'Clown Face' Makeup." *Medium*, September 12, 2019. https://libbyjanecharleston.medium.com/the-truth-behind-queen-elizabeths-white-clown-face-makeup-c0507a178bd5.

Chilcote, Paul, ed. *Her Own Story: Autobiographical Portraits of Early Methodist Women*. Nashville: Abingdon, 2001.

Church of England. *Catechism of the Church of England (1662)*. Edited by John Baskerville. Cambridge: Cambridge University Press, 1962.

Clarke, Adam. *Memoirs of the Wesley Family*. New York: Lane & Tippett, 1848.

Corlet, Molly. "Between Colony and Metropole." In *Black British History: New Persepecives*, edited by Hakim Adi, 37–51. London: Zed, 2019.

Cornfield, P. J. "Class and Name and Number in Eighteenth-Century Britain." *History* 72.234 (February 1987) 36–61.

Cragg, Gerald. *Reason and Authority in the Eighteenth Century*. Cambridge: Cambridge University Press, 1964.

Cugoano, Ottabah. *Thoughts and Sentiments on the Evil and Wicked Traffic of the Slavery and Commerce of the Human Species Humbly Submitted to the Inhabitants of Great-Britain, by Ottobah Cugoano a Native of Africa*. London: NA, 1787.

Day, Felicity. "'A Nation Addicted to Gaming': The Georgians' Crackdown on Addictive Betting." *History Extra*, August 20, 2018. http://www.historyextra.com/period/georgian/gaming-gambling-betting-addiction-g.

Defoe, Daniel. *Conjugal Lewdness, or Matrimonial Whoredom*. London: T. Warner, 1727.

———. *Everybody's Business Is Nobody's Business: or Private Abuses, Public Grievances, Exemplified in the Pride, Insolence, and Exhorbitant Wages of Our Women, Servants, and Footmen*. London: W. Meadows, 1725.

———. *The Great Law of Subordination Consider'd; Or the Insolence and Unsufferable Behaviour of Servants in England Duly Enquir'd Into; Illustrated with a Great Variety of Examples, Historical Cases, and Remarkable Stories of the Behaviour of Some Particular Servants . . . in Ten Familiar Letters*. London: S. Harding Lewis, 1724.

———. *The Shortest Way with the Dissenters or Proposals for the Establishment of the Church*. London: NA, 1702.

———. *The True-Born English Man: A Satire*. Leeds: Alice Mann, 1701.

Dillon, Frank. *Gin: The Much-Lamented Death of Madam Geneva*. Boston: Justin Charles, 2003.

Disney, John. *An Essay upon the Execution of the Laws Against Morality and Prophaneness*. London: Joseph Downing, 1710.

Disraeli, Benjamin. *Sybil: The Two Nations*. 2 vols. London: Henry Colburn, 1845.

Donovan, Robert Kent. "The Military Origins of the Roman Catholic Relief Programme of 1778." *Historical Journal* 28 (March 1985) 79–102.

Dryden, John. "Absalom and Achitophel (1681)." *Poetry Foundation*. https://www.poetryfoundation.org/poems/44172/absalom-and-achitophel.

Ecclestone, Edward. *Noah's Flood, or the Destruction of the World: An Opera.* London: M. Clark, 1679.

Edwards, Maldwin. *After Wesley: A Study of the Social and Political Influence of Methodism in the Middle Period, 1791–1849.* London: Epworth, 1935.

Edwards, Paul. "The History of Black People in Britain." *History Today* 31.9 (September 1981). http://www.historytoday.com/archive/history-black-people-britain.

Eldridge, Lisa. *Face Paint: The Story of Make-up.* New York: Abrams, 2015.

Emsley, Clive, et al. "Black Communities." *The Proceedings of the Old Bailey,* December 1, 2012. https://www.oldbaileyonline.org/static/Black.jsp.

———. "London History—A Population History of London." *The Proceedings of the Old Bailey,* April 30, 2022. https://www.oldbaileyonline.org/static/Population-history-of-london.jsp.

Evans, Frederick. *The State of the Poor; or an History of the Labouring Class in England from the Conquest to the Present Day.* 3 vols. London: J. Davis, 1797.

Ferling, John. "Myths of the American Revolution." *Smithsonian Magazine,* January 2010. https://www.smithsonianmag.com/history/myths-of-the-american-revolution-10941835/.

Field, Clive. "Counting Religion in England and Wales: The Long Eighteenth Century, c. 1680–1840." *Journal of Ecclesiastical History* 63 (October 2012) 693–720.

———. "Eighteenth-Century Religious Statistics." *British Religion in Numbers,* September 21, 2012. http://www.brin.ac.uk/eighteenth-century-religious-statistics.

———. "A Schilling for Queen Elizabeth: The Era of State Regulation of the Church Attendance in England." *Journal of Church and State* 50.2 (Spring 2008) 213–53.

Fielding, Henry. *An Enquiry into the Causes of the Late Increase of Robbers, etc. With Some Proposals for Remedy This Growing Evil.* London: A. Millar, 1751.

Finley, Jeanne Terance. *Three Simple Rules for Christian Living.* Nashville: Abingdon, 2008.

Fisher, James. *The Westminster Assembly's Shorter Catechism Explained, by Way of Question and Answer.* 4th ed. Philadelphia: William Young, 1840.

Forsaith, Peter. *Image, Identity, and John Wesley.* New York: Routledge, 2018.

Frazier, Tony. "The Invention of Mungo: Race and Representation in the Eighteenth-Century Atlantic World." *International Journal of the Arts and Humanities* 5.2 (April 2019) 17–27.

French, G. S. "Ruckle, Barbara (Heck)." In *Dictionary of Canadian Biography, Volume 5 (1801–1820),* edited by James Nicholson. 22 vols. http://www.biographi.ca/en/bio/ruckle_barbara_5E.html.

Fryer, Peter. *Staying Power: The History of Black People in Britain.* London: Pluto, 2018.

Gates, Henry Louis. *The Trials of Phillis Wheatley.* New York: Basic Civitas, 2003.

Gee, Joshua. `. London: Samuel Buckley, 1729.

George, Dorothy. *England in Transition.* Baltimore: Penguin, 1953.

Gerard, Kent, and Gert Heckma, eds. *The Pursuit of Sodomy: Male Homosexuality in Renaissance and Enlightenment Europe.* New York: Harrington Park, 1989.

Gerzina, Gretchen Holbrook. *Black London.* New Brunswick, NJ: Rutgers University Press, 1995.

"Getting the Vote." *National Archives.* http://www.nationalarchives.gov.uk/pathways/citizenship/struggle_democracy/getting_vote.htm.

Gilbert, Alan. *Religion and Society in Industrial England: Church, Chapel, and Social Change*. London: Longman, 1976.

Gillard, Derek. *Education in England: A History*. London: printed by the author, 2018.

Gleckner, Robert. *Gray Agonistes*. Baltimore: John Hopkins University Press, 1997.

Goldenberg, David. *Black and Slave: The History of the Curse of Ham*. Berlin: DeGruyter, 2017.

Gother, John. *A Papist Misrepresented and Represented*. London: James Marcus Corker, 1683.

Griffin, Marvin. *Latitudinarianism in the 17th Century of England*. London: Brill, 1992.

Grubb, Farley. "The Fatherless and Friendless: Factors Influencing the Flow of English Emigrant Servants." *Journal of Economic History* 52.1 (March 1992) 85–108.

Hamilton, Carol V. "Why Did Jefferson Change 'Property' to the 'Pursuit of Happiness?'" *History News Network*, January 27, 2008. https://historynewsnetwork.org/article/46460.

Harvey, Karen. "The Century of Sex." *Historical Journal* 45 (Fall 2002) 899–916.

Haynes, Clare. "The Culture of Judgment: Art and Anti-Catholicism in England, c. 1660–1760." *Historical Research* 78 (November 2005) 483–505.

Heales, Alfred. *The History and Law of Church Seats or Pews*. 2 vols. London: Butterworths, 1872.

Heitzenrater, Richard. *Wesley and the People Called Methodists*. Nashville: Abingdon, 2013.

Higgenbotham, Peter. "Education in the Workhouse." *Workhouse*, 2021. http://www.workhouses.org.uk/education/workhouse.shtml.

Hilderbrandt, Franz, and Oliver Beckerlegge, eds. "Preface." In *A Collection of Hymns for the Use of the People Called Methodists*, by John Wesley, 7:73–77. Vol. 7 of *The Works of John Wesley*. Nashville: Abingdon, 1989.

Hill, Harvey. "The Law of Nature Revived: Christianity and Natural Religion in the Sermons of John Tillotson." *Journal of Anglican and Episcopal History* 70.2 (June 2001) 169–89.

Hitchcock, Tim, et al. "Workhouses." *London Lives*, March 2018. http://londonlives.org/static/Workhouses.jsp.

Hoeveler, Diane. "Anti-Catholicism and the Gothic Imagery: The Historical and Literary Contexts." In *Religion in the Age of Enlightenment*, edited by Brett C. McInelly, 1–35. New York: AMS, 2013.

Hudson, Chuck. "Pastimes in the Georgian Era." *The Historic Interpreter*, November 11, 2014. http://historicinterpreter.wordpress.com/2014/11/11/entertainment-in-the-georgian-era.

Hume, David. "Of National Characters." In *Essays Moral, Political and Literary*, 197–214. London: T. Cadell, 1747, 1777. https://davidhume.org/texts/empl1/nc

Jackson, Francis, ed. *An Index to the Memoirs, Obituary Notices, and Recent Deaths, Together with the References to the Local Histories of Methodism*. Westcliff-on-Sea, UK: Gage Postal, 1985.

Jackson, Thomas. *The Life of Charles Wesley, A.M.* New York: Lane & Sandford, 1842.

———. *The Lives of Early Methodist Preachers*. 6 vols. London: Wesleyan Methodist Book-Room, 1878.

Jennings, David. *A Vindication of the Scripture-Doctrine of Original Sin*. London: R. Hett, 1740.

Jenys, Soame. *Free Inquiry into the Nature and the Origin of Evil, in Six Letters*. London: R. J. Dolney, 1758.

Job, Rueben. *Three Simple Rules: A Wesleyan Way of Living*. Nashville: Abingdon, 2007.

Johnson, Samuel. "London: A Poem in Imitation of the Third Satire of Juvenal." In *A Collection of Poems*, edited by Richard Dodsley. London: J. Hughes, 1758. https://rpo.library.utoronto.ca/content/london-poem-imitation-third-satire-juvenal.

Jones, Brad A. "'In Favour of Popery': Patriotism, Protestantism, and the Gordon Riots in the Revolutionary British Atlantic." *Journal of British Studies* 52.1 (January 2013) 79–102.

Jones, Pip, and Rita Youseph. *The Black Population of Bristol in the Eighteenth Century*. Bristol: University of Bristol Press, 1994.

King, Peter, and John Carter. "Black People and the Criminal Justice System: Prejudice and Practice in Later Eighteenth- and Early Nineteenth-Century London." *Historical Research* 88.239 (February 2015) 100–24.

Knight, Jude. "The Rakehell in Fact and Fiction." *Dirty, Sexy History*, October 27, 2016. https://dirtysexyhistory.com/2016/10/27/the-rakehell-in-fact-and-fiction/.

Laqueur, Thomas. *Making Sex: Body and Gender from the Greeks to Freud*. Cambridge: Harvard University Press, 1990.

Laqueur, W. T. *Religion and Respectability: Sunday Schools and Working-Class Culture*. New Haven: Yale University Press, 1976.

Lavington, George. *The Enthusiasm of Methodists and Papists Comp'd, in Three Parts*. London: J. and P. Knapton, 1754.

Leger, J. A. *John Wesley's Last Love*. London: J. M. Dent, 1910.

Lein, Clayton D. "Jonathan Swift and the Population of Ireland." *Eighteenth-Century Studies* 8 (Summer 1975) 431–53.

Lloyd, Gareth. "'Running after Strange Women': An Insight into John Wesley's Troubled Marriage from a Newly Discovered Manuscript Written by His Wife." *Proceedings of the Wesley Historical Society* 53 (May 2002) 169–74.

———. "Sarah Perrin (1721–1787): Early Methodist Exhorter." *Methodist History* 41.2 (April 2003) 79–88.

Lobody, Diane. "A Wren Just Bursting Its Shell: Catherine Livingston Garrettson's Ministry of Public Domesticity." In *Spirituality and Social Responsibility*, edited by Rosemary Keller, 19–40. Nashville: Abingdon, 1993.

Locke, John. *An Essay Concerning Human Understanding*. 4 vols. London: Hale, 1690.

Lyles, Albert M. *Methodism Mocked*. London: Epworth, 1960.

Madan, Martin. *Thoughts on Executive Justice, With Respect to Our Criminal Laws, Particularly on the Circuits*. London: J. Dodsley, 1785.

Maddox, Randy, and Timothy Underhill. "Untangling the Tangled Web: Charles Wesley and Elizabeth Story." *Wesley and Methodist Studies* 6.2 (2016) 175–83.

Magennis, Eoins. "The Present State of Ireland, 1749." *Irish Historical Studies* 36 (November 2009) 581–97.

Mahon, Charles. "Key Dates in Census, Statistics and Registration: Great Britain 1000–1899." *The Potteries*. http://www.thepotteries.org/dates/census.htm.

Mandeville, Bernard. *The Fable of the Bees; or Private Vices, Public Benefits, 1732*. Published by Jonathan Bennett, 2017.

Maser, Frederick. *Seven Sisters in Search of Love*. Rutland, VT: Academy, 1988.

Mathias, Peter. "The Social Structure of the Eighteenth Century: A Calculation by Joseph Massie." *Economic History Review* 10 (1958) 30–45.

McInerney, Timothy. "The Better Sort: Nobility and Human Variety in Eighteenth-Century Great Britain." *Eighteenth-Century Studies* 38.1 (March 2015) 47–63.

McNeil, Peter. *Pretty Gentlemen*. New Haven: Yale University Press, 2018.

Miskelly, Elizabeth Raigan Vowell. "Restoration: A Wesleyan Model of Recovery." DMin diss., Duke University Divinity School, 2016.

Molineux, Catherine. "Hogarth's Fashionable Slaves: Moral Corruption in Eighteenth-Century London." *English Literary History* 72.2 (Summer 2005) 495–520.

Montagu, Mary Wortley. *Letters from the Right Honourable Lady Mary Wortley Montagu*. Edited by R. Brunly Johnson. London: J. M. Dent, 1906.

Moore, Arthur Allen, III. "Catherine 'Kitty' Livingston Garrettson." *Find a Grave*, February 15, 2010. https://www.findagrave.com/memorial/48178792/catherine-garrettson.

Morgan, William Thomas. "An Eighteenth-Century Election in England." *Political Science Quarterly* 37.4 (December 1922) 585–604.

Myers, Robert Manson. "Mrs. Delany: An Eighteenth-Century Handelian." *Musical Quarterly* 32.1 (1946) 12–36.

Nelson, James. *An Essay on the Government of Children: Under Three General Heads, viz. Health, Manners, and Education*. London: R. and J. Dodsely, 1763.

Neuburg, Victor E. *Popular Education in Eighteenth-Century England*. London: Woburn, 1971.

Nind, John Newton. *Mary Clark Nind and Her Work: By Her Children*. Chicago: Methodist Mission Society, 1906.

North, Eric. *Early Methodist Philanthropy*. New York: Methodist Book Concern, 1914.

Norton, Rictor. "The Macaroni Club: Homosexual Scandals in 1772." *Homosexuality in Eighteenth-Century England*, December 19, 2004. http://rictornorton.co.uk/eighteen/macaroni.htm.

———. "The Raid on Mother Clap's Molly House." *Homosexuality in Eighteenth-Century England*, February 2005. http://rictornorton.co.uk/eighteen/mother.htm.

O'Brien, George. *An Economic History of Ireland in the Eighteenth Century*. London: Maunse, 1918.

O'Brien, Richard Barry. *Studies in the History of Ireland, 1649–1775*. London: MacMillian, 1903.

Orwell, George. *England, Your England*. New York: Penguin, 1982.

Outler, Albert. *Theology in the Wesleyan Spirit*. Nashville: Tidings, 1975.

Parratt, Catriona. "Robert W. Malcolmson's 'Popular Recreations in English Society, 1700–1850,' an Appreciation." *Journal of Sport History* 29.2 (Summer 2002) 312–23.

Payne, Dianne. "London's Charity School Children: The 'Scum of the Parish'?" *British Journal for Eighteenth-Century Studies* 29 (2006) 383–97.

Perkin, Harold. *The Origins of Modern English Society*. London: Routlege, 1969.

Petrie, Charles. *The Four Georges: A Revaluation of the Period From 1714–1830*. London: Eyre & Spottswoode, 1935.

Pope, Alexander. *An Essay on Man: Moral Essays and Satires*. Edited by Henry Morley. London: Cassels, 1891.

Porter, Roy. *English Society in the Eighteenth Century*. London: Penguin, 1982.

Rack, Henry. "'But Lord, Let It Be Betsy!' Love in Early Methodism." *Proceedings of the Wesley Historical Society* 53 (February 2001) 1–13.

————. *Reasonable Enthusiast: John Wesley and the Rise of Methodism*. Philadelphia: Epworth, 2014.

Rogers, Nicholas. "Popular Protest in Early Hanoverian London." *Past and Present Society* 79.1 (May 1979) 70–100.

Ross, David, ed. "Henry VIII's 1534 Act of Supremacy (1534)—Full Text." *Britain Express*. https://www.britainexpress.com/History/tudor/supremacy-henry-text.htm.

Salmon, D. "Work of the Charity Schools." In *The Encyclopedia and Dictionary of Education*, edited by F. Watson, 3:294–95. 3 vols. London: Pittman and Sons, 1921

Sancho, Ignatius. *Letters of the Late Ignatius Sancho, an African*. Edited by Joseph Jerkyll. 2 vols. London: J. Nicholas, 1782.

Sandhu, Sukhdev. "The First Black Britons." *BBC History*, February 17, 2011. www.bbc.co.uk/history/british/empire_seapower/black_britons_01.shtml.

Sandys, George. *A Relation of a Journey Begun An. Dom. 1610*. London: W. Barrett, 1615.

Schiesbinger, Londa. "The Anatomy of Differences: Race and Sex in Eighteenth-Century Science." *Eighteenth-Century Studies* 23 (Summer 1990) 385–405.

Schlenther, Boyd S. "Whitefield, George, 1714–1770." In *Oxford Dictionary of National Biography* I:2981. https://doi.org/10.1093/ref:odnb/29281.

Segal, David. "That Diss Song Known as 'Yankee Doodle.'" *New York Times*, July 1, 2017. https://www.nytimes.com/2017/07/01/sunday-review/that-diss-song-known-as-yankee-doodle.html.

Sherwin, Oscar. "Crime and Punishment in England of the Eighteenth Century." *American Journal of Economics and Sociology* 5.2 (January 1946) 169–99.

Shipley, Joseph. *The Origins of English Words: A Discursive Dictionary of Into-European Root*. Baltimore: Johns Hopkins University Press, 1984.

Shoemaker, Robert B. "The London 'Mob' in the Early Eighteenth Century." *Journal of British Studies* 25.3 (July 1987) 273–304.

Small, Stephen. "Reconstructing the Black Past." *Albion* 29 (Winter 1997) 689–91.

Smith, John Q. "Occupational Groups among the Early Methodists of the Keighley Circuit." *Church History* 57.2 (June 1988) 187–96.

Solomonson, Lesley Jacobs. *Gin: A Global History*. London: Reakton, 2012.

South, Robert. *Twelve Sermons and Discourses on Several Subjects and Occasions*. London: Jonah Rowyer, 1717.

Steele, Anthony. *History of Methodism*. London: George Vickers, 1857.

Steinberg, Jessica. *Seven Deadly Sins of Prostitution: Perceptions of Prostitutes in Eighteenth-Century London*. Ottawa: University of Ottawa Press, 2015.

Stetzer, Ed. "If It Doesn't Stem Its Decline, Mainline Protestantism Has Just 23 Easters Left." *Washington Post*, April 28, 2017. https://www.washingtonpost.com/news/acts-of-faith/wp/2017/04/28/if-it-doesnt-stem-its-decline-mainline-protestantism-has-just-23-easters-left.

Stone, Lawrence. *The Family, Sex, and Marriage in England, 1500–1800*. New York: Harper and Row, 1971.

————. "Literacy and Education in England, 1640–1900." *Past and Present* 42 (1969) 69–139.

Sugden, Edward. "A Wesley Class Register." *Proceedings of the Wesley Historical Society* 12.4 (December 1919) 75–77.

Swift, Jonathan. "Baucis and Philemon." *Eighteenth-Century Poetry Archive*. https://www.eighteenthcenturypoetry.org/works/psw11-w0060.shtml.

———. *Miscellanies*. London: John Morphew, 1713.

———. "The Present Miserable State of Conditions in Ireland." In vol. 7, *The Prose Works of Jonathan Swift*, edited by Temple Scott, 7:153–65. 12 vols. London: Bell and Sons, 1905.

Sykes, Norman. *Church and State in England in the Eighteenth Century*. Hamden, CT: Archon, 1962.

Szreter, Simon, and Kevin Sierna. "The Pox in Boswell's London: An Estimate of the Extent of Syphilis Infection in the Metropolis in the 1770s." *Economic History Review* 74.2 (May 2021) 372–99.

Taylor, John James. "Church and State in England in the Mid-Eighteenth Century." PhD diss., Jesus College, Cambridge University, 1987.

Telford, John. *Two West-End Chapels, or Sketches of London Methodism from Wesley's Day*. London: Epworth, 1886.

Thom, Danielle. "Sawney's Defence: Anti-Catholicism, Consumption, and Performance in 18th-Century Britain." *V&A Online Journal* 7 (Summer 2015). http://www.vam.ac.uk/content/journals/research-journal/issue-no.-7-autumn-2015/sawneys-defence-anti-catholicism,-consumption-and-performance-in-18th-century-britain/.

Thomas, J. D. "The Case of Somersett from Freedom's Journal." *Accessible Archives*, November 30, 2012. https://www.accessible-archives.com/2012/11/case-of-somersett-from-freedoms-journal/.

Tillotson, John. *The Works of the Rev. Dr. John Tillotson, Lord Archbishop of Canterbury*. 12 vols. London: R. Wade, 1743.

Trusler, John. *Three Short Letters to the People of England, Proving the Public Grievances Complained of to be Ideal*. London, 1790; Ann Arbor: Text Creation Partnership, 2011. https://quod.lib.umich.edu/e/ecco/004862597.0001.000?rgn=main;view=fulltext.

Tyson, John R. *Assist Me to Proclaim: the Life and Hymns of Charles Wesley*. Grand Rapids: Eerdmans, 2007.

———. *Charles Wesley: A Reader*. Oxford: Oxford Univeristy Press, 1989.

———. "Charles Wesley, Evangelist: The Unpublished Newcastle Journal." *Methodist History* 25.1 (Oct. 1986) 41–61.

———. "An Instrument for Sally: Charles Wesley's Shorthand Biography of John Davis." *Methodist History* 30.2 (January 1991) 103–8.

———. "Lady Huntingdon's Reformation." *Church History* 64.4 (December 1995) 580–93.

———. "Lady Huntingdon, Religion, and Race." *Methodist History* 50 (October 2011) 28–40.

———. "'A Poor, Vile Sinner': Lady Huntingdon's Language of Weakness and Deference." *Methodist History* 37.2 (January 1991) 107–19.

———. "Why Did John Wesley Fail? A Reappraisal of Wesley's Evangelical Economics." *Methodist History* 25.3 (April 1997) 176–88.

United Methodist Church. *The Book of Discipline*. Nashville: United Methodist, 2016.

Vickers, Jason E. *Wesley: A Guide for the Perplexed*. London: T. & T. Clark, 2009.

Voth, Hans-Jochim. "Time and Work in Eighteenth-Century London." *Journal of Economic History* 58.1 (March 1998) 29–58.

Walsh, John. "Methodism and the Mob in the Eighteenth Century." *Studies in Church History* 8 (1972) 213–27.

———. "Methodism at the End of the Eighteenth Century." In *A History of the Methodist Church in Great Britain,* edited by Davies and Rupp, eds., 1:275–315. 4 vols. London: Epworth, 1965.

Walsh, Patrick. "A New Edmund Burke Letter from 1778." *Eighteenth-Century Ireland* 24 (2009) 159–63.

Ward, Reginald. *The Protestant Evangelical Awakening.* Cambridge: Cambridge University Press, 1992.

Warrick, Susan. "'She Diligently Followed Every Good Work': Mary Mason and the New York Female Missionary Society." *Methodist History* 34.4 (July 1996) 214–29.

Waters, Michael. "The Macaroni in 'Yankee Doodle' Is Not What You Think." *Atlas Obscura,* August 24, 2016. http://www.atlasobscura.com/articles/the-macaroni-in-yankee-doodle-is-not-what-you-think.

Welter, Barbara. "The Cult of True Womanhood." *American Quarterly* 18.2 (Summer 1966) 151–74.

Wesley, Charles. *Hymns for Those that Seek and Those that have Redemption in the Blood of Jesus Christ.* London: Strahan, 1747.

———. *The Journal of Charles Wesley.* 2 vols. Edited by Thomas Jackson. London: Wesleyan Conference, 1849.

———. *The Letters of Charles Wesley.* Edited by Kenneth Newport and Gareth Lloyd. Oxford: Oxford University Press, 2013.

———. *The Manuscript Journal of the Reverend Charles Wesley, M.A.* Edited by Kenneth Newport et al. 2 vols. Nashville: Abingdon, 2007.

———. *The Representative Verse of Charles Wesley.* Edited by Frank Baker. Nashville: Abingdon, 1962.

———. *The Sermons of Charles Wesley: A Critical Edition with Introduction and Notes.* Edited by Kenneth Newport. Oxford: Oxford University Press, 2001.

———. *The Unpublished Poetry of Charles Wesley.* Edited by S. T. Kimbrough and Oliver Beckerlegge. 3 vols. Nashville: Abingdon, 1990.

Wesley, Charles, and John Wesley. *The Poetical Works of John and Charles Wesley.* Edited by George Osborn. 13 vols. London: Wesleyan Conference, 1886.

Wesley, John. *The Appeals to Men of Reason and Religion and Certain Related Open Letters.* Vol. 11 of *The Works of John Wesley.* Edited by Gerald Cragg. Oxford: Clarendon, 1975.

———, ed. *The Christian Library: Extracts from and Abridgments of the Choicest Pieces of Practical Divinity Which Have Been Published in the English Tongue.* 50 vols. London: Dutton, 1821.

———. *A Collection of Hymns for the Use of the People Called Methodists.* Vol. 7 of *The Works of John Wesley.* Edited by Franz Hilderbrandt and Oliver Beckerlegge Nashville: Abingdon, 1989.

———. *Doctrinal and Controversial Treatises I.* Vol. 12 of *The Works of John Wesley.* Edited by Randy Maddox. Nashville: Abingdon, 2012.

———. *Doctrinal and Controversial Treatises II.* Vol. 13 of *The Works of John Wesley.* Edited by Paul Chilcote and Kenneth Collins. Nashville: Abingdon, 2013.

———. *Explanatory Notes Upon the Old and New Testament.* 4 vols. Salem, OH: Schmul, 1755.

————. *Journal and Diaries*. Edited by W. Reginald Ward and Richard P. Heitzenrater. 7 vols. Nashville, Abingdon, 1988–2003.

————. *The Journal of Rev. John Wesley A.M.* Edited by Nehemiah Curnock. 8 vols. London: Richard Culley, 1910.

————. *The Letters of the Rev. John Wesley*. Edited by John Telford. 8 vols. London: Epworth, 1931.

————. *Letters II*. Vol. 20 of *The Works of John Wesley*. Edited by Frank Baker. Oxford: Clarendon, 1982.

————. *Letters III*. Vol. 27 of *The Works of John Wesley*. Edited by Ted Campbell. Nashville: Abingdon, 2015.

————. *The Methodist Societies*. Vol. 9 of *The Works of John Wesley*. Edited by Rupert Davies. Nashville: Abingdon, 1989.

————. *Sermons*. Edited by Albert Outler. 4 vols. Nashville: Abingdon, 1987.

————. *The Works of John Wesley*. Edited by Thomas Jackson. 14 vols. London: Wesleyan Conference, 1872.

Wesley, Susanna. *The Complete Writings*. Edited by Charles Wallace. Oxford: Oxford University Press, 1997.

White, Jonathan. "The 'Slow But Sure Poyson,' the Representation of Gin and Its Drinkers." *Journal of British Studies* 42.1 (January 2003) 35–64.

Whitefield, George. *The Works of the Rev. George Whitefield, M.A.* 4 vols. London: Dilly, 1771.

Whiteley, John. *Wesley's England*. London: Epworth, 1938.

"Who Were the Black Loyalists?" *Nova Scotia Museum*, 2001. https://novascotia.ca/museum/blackloyalists/who.htm.

Wilder, Franklin. *The Methodist Riots*. New York: Todd & Honeywell, 1981.

Wiles, R. M. "Middle-Class Literacy in Eighteenth-Century England." In *Studies in the Eighteenth Century*, edited by R. F. Brissenden, 49–66. Toronto: University of Toronto Press, 1968.

Willis, Andre C. "The Impact of David Hume's Thought about Race for the Stance on Slavery and His Concept of Religion." *Hume Studies* 42 (April/September 2016) 213–30.

Wilson, Thomas. *Distilled Spirituous Liquors: The Bane of the Nation*. London: J. Roberts, 1736.

Withrow, W. H. *Barbara Heck: A Story of Early Methodism*. London: C. H. Kelly, 1897.

General Index

Scripture Index